Health Insurance Nuts and Bolts

Study Guide

For Use in the AHIP Course
*Fundamentals of
Health Insurance, Part B*

America's Health Insurance Plans
Washington, DC 20004

ISBN 1-879143-52-6

Health Insurance Nuts and Bolts

Study Guide

For Use in the AHIP Course
*Fundamentals of
Health Insurance, Part B*

CONTENTS

HOW TO USE THIS STUDY GUIDE

This study guide has two purposes:

- to indicate to the student what information and concepts are most important, and

- to help the student learn and understand that material.

The study guide should be used by those taking the examination for the AHIP course *Fundamentals of Health Insurance, Part B.* It is also recommended to anyone who wants to thoroughly master the material presented in *Health Insurance Nuts and Bolts.*

If I know the answers to all of the questions in the study guide, will I pass the AHIP examination?

The study guide covers all the important points asked about in the examination. So, although we cannot make any guarantees, if you truly know and understand all of these points, you should pass the exam without difficulty.

Of course, the questions on the exam will not be the same as those in the study guide. They may be phrased differently, they may ask about a different aspect of the same point, or they may require you to apply your knowledge to solve a problem. This means you must really learn the material, not just go through the study guide once.

What is the best way to use the study guide?

We recommend the following approach:

- Read a chapter of the textbook.

- Read the questions in the study guide and answer them to yourself.

- As you answer the questions, check the correct answers at the end of each chapter.

- Mark any questions you were not able to answer correctly and review them.

- If you do not understand an answer, reread the corresponding section of the textbook.

- If you miss a lot of the questions for a section, reread that section.

- Before you take the test, thoroughly review all questions to make sure you can answer them correctly.

If I do not understand an answer and want to reread the textbook, how can I find the right page?

The title of each section of the study guide includes the page numbers of the corresponding section of the textbook.

Do I need to write down the answers to the questions?

No. As long as you check your answers against the correct answers, you do not need to write them out.

Of course, everyone has different studying styles, and some students may prefer to write out their answers. However, it should be kept in mind that, because the study guide covers all the important points in the textbook, there are many questions. Writing out the answer to every question may be very time consuming. If you like to write, you may want to consider a compromise approach, such as writing out only the information you find particularly difficult to remember or that you want to organize and clarify for yourself.

Why are vocabulary questions marked with an icon? ♦

This is strictly for your convenience. Some students like to study all the vocabulary of a chapter at one time so they can compare and contrast terms. The use of the icon enables you to find all vocabulary items easily while at the same time allowing those items to be presented along with the information and concepts they relate to, instead of separately and out of context at the end of the chapter.

What are the practice exam questions at the end of the study guide?

These are questions in the multiple-choice format of the actual examination. The purpose of including them is to enable students to become accustomed to this format. Students should also be aware that they can take an online pretest (a practice exam with immediate scoring) at *www.insuranceeducation.org.*

FREQUENTLY ASKED QUESTIONS ABOUT THE EXAMINATION

What material is covered in the examination?

The 17 chapters of the textbook *Health Insurance Nuts and Bolts.*

What is the format of the questions of the exam?

All questions are four-part multiple choice. See the practice exam questions at the end of the study guide for examples.

A few questions are multiple-option multiple choice. An example:

Medical expense policies usually have
I.   deductibles.
II.   coinsurance.
III. overall maximums

a. I and II only.

b. I and III only.

c. II and III only.

d. I, II, and III.

(The correct answer is d.)

What are application questions?

Questions that require you to apply your knowledge. An example:

John has an insurance policy with a $500 deductible. He incurs an expense of $1,200, which is covered by the policy. If this is his first covered expense this year, how much will his insurance company reimburse him?

a. $500.

b. $700.

c. $1,200.

d. $1,700.

(The correct answer is b.)

You should be able to apply your knowledge of how a deductible works to answer the question.

How many questions are on the test and how much time do I have?

There are 75 questions. You have two hours.

Are there questions on the statistics and numbers in the textbook?

Yes, but not very many. In the case of some simple and important numbers, the exact figure must be known. In other cases, an approximate idea of the number is sufficient. The questions of the study guide serve as an indication of what numbers we consider important and what degree of precision is required. However, we will provide two examples to illustrate our general approach to numbers.

- Under HIPAA, the look-back period for preexisting conditions is six months. The student is expected to know this number.

- About 70 percent of Americans have private health insurance. The student is expected to have only an approximate idea of this number. The question would not ask whether the percentage is 65, 70, 75, or 80 percent, but rather whether it is 25, 50, 70, or 95 percent, or perhaps whether a minority, about half, a majority, or nearly all Americans have such coverage.

Is information from figures and tables covered in the exam?

Yes, information from the figures and tables of the 17 chapters are covered, but the basic facts, not the details, are tested. Take the example of a graph comparing different kinds of insurance in terms of number of policies sold. The exam question might ask which kind is most popular. It would not ask how many policies of a particular kind were sold. As with number questions, the study guide should be used as an indication of what information is considered important.

I have a lot of experience in insurance. Can I pass the exam without reading the textbook or studying?

Possibly, but you should be aware that the examination is based on the most common practices in the insurance industry. What your company does may differ. The safest approach is to read the textbook and see if you can answer the questions in the study guide. This will go very quickly if you already have a lot of knowledge.

1 THE ADMINISTRATION OF GROUP HEALTH INSURANCE PLANS

Introduction (Page 1)

1. Some insurance operations are handled differently from company to company because of differences in company _____, _____, and _____.

Insurer Administration and Policyholder Administration (Pages 2–3)

2. Individual health insurance policies are administered by (the insurer / the policyholder / either or both).

3. Group health insurance plans are administered by (the insurer / the policyholder / either or both).   .

4. If a group health insurance plan is **self-administered**, the (insurer / employer) handles most administrative functions.

5. **Self-accounting** is (the same as / different from) self-administration.

6. In self-administered plans, three of the following four functions are usually performed by the employer, but one may be performed by either the employer or the insurer. Which one?

   - Administering claims,

   - enrolling employees,

   - maintaining employee records, or

   - preparing premium statements.

7. In some self-administered plans, the insurer as well as the employer maintains records on individual employees. Whether this is done is determined by which party handles_____

8. In self-administered plans, what role does the insurer take in each of these three areas?

   a. Training.

   b. Operational procedures.

   c. Unusual circumstances.

9. In general, a self-administering employer pays (higher / lower) premiums for the same benefits than an employer with an insurer-administered plan.

10. What two questions generally determine whether an employer chooses insurer administration or self-administration for its group health insurance plan?

11. Self-administration is more common for (large / small) groups.

12. (Most / Only a few) insurers administer all their plans themselves.

Auditing Self-Administered Plans (Pages 3–4)

♦ 13. **External** or **internal audit**?

   a. Takes place in the employer's facilities.

   b. Takes place in the insurer's offices.

   c. A limited and informal process.

   d. A formal process.

   e. Performed by a trained auditor.

   f. Performed by insurer personnel who are not professional auditors.

14. What are the two main questions addressed by an external audit?

15. In an external audit, why would an auditor perform each of the following actions?

   a. Examining employee enrollment cards.

   b. Counting the enrollment cards.

   c. Reviewing employee records.

   d. Making spot checks of claims.

16. An internal audit consists primarily of reviewing_____.

17. In addition to the discovery and correction of errors, what purpose do audits serve?

18. Whether an insurer audits its self-administered plans depends on two factors. What are they?

Self-Insured Plans (Pages 4–5)

♦ 19. In a **self-insured group plan**, coverage is provided and financial risk assumed by (the employer / an insurer).

♦ 20. In a **fully insured group plan**, coverage is provided and financial risk assumed by (the employer / an insurer).

21. In a self-insured group plan, claims are paid from (insurer funds / employer funds).

22. In a fully insured group plan, claims are paid from (insurer funds / employer funds).

23. Insurers may be involved in self-insured plans by providing _____ to partially self-insured plans and _____ to fully self-insured plans.

♦ 24. In a **partially self-insured plan**, the employer assumes most of the risk of paying health care benefits to its employees, but it buys some coverage from an insurer to protect itself from (unusually high levels of claims / periods in which it does not make a profit).

♦ 25. In a **minimum premium plan (MPP)** the employer pays for its employees' normal level of claims, but if claims rise above that level, the insurer pays (all claims / the excess).

Third-Party Administrators (TPAs) (Pages 5–6)

♦ 26. A **third-party administrator (TPA)** is a firm that administers an insurance plan but is neither _____ nor _____.

27. Orinoco Drilling Company has a self-insured plan but hires a TPA to run it. Orinoco probably lacks the _____ and/or the _____ needed to administer coverage.

28. TPAs are (always / sometimes / never) insurance companies.

29. TPAs administer (self-insured plans only / fully insured plans only / both).

30. Charley's Cheeses Inc. purchases a group plan from Shawnee Insurance and hires a TPA to administer the plan. What is the probable reason for this arrangement?

♦ 31. **ASO** stands for _____. In an ASO, the TPA handles _____.

♦ 32. **CSO** stands for _____. In a CSO, the TPA handles _____.

33. Legally, the important distinction of an ASO is that the insurer or other business acting as a TPA does not provide

34. In an ASO arrangement in which the TPA is an insurer, there (is / is not) an insurance contract between the employer and the insurer.

35. ASO arrangements are normally subject to the requirements of (state insurance departments / ERISA / both).

Summary (Page 6)

36. Match the descriptions below with these types of group plan administration:

- Fully insured, insurer-administered plan.

- Fully insured, self-administered plan.

- Self-insured plan with a third-party administrator.

- Self-insured plan with no third-party administrator.

- Partially self-insured plan.

a. The employer provides its own coverage, but an insurer or other firm administers the plan.

b. The insurer provides coverage, but the employer administers the plan.

c. The employer and the insurer both provide coverage, and the employer may administer the plan itself or hire a third-party administrator.

d. The insurer both provides coverage and administers the plan.

e. employer both provides its own coverage and administers the plan.

Answers

1. Size, products, and organizational structure.

2. The insurer.

3. Either or both.

4. Employer.

5. The same as.

6. Administering claims.

7. Claims. (If the employer handles claims, the insurer does not keep its own employee records. If the insurer handles claims, it keeps such records.)

8. a. The insurer trains employer personnel when the plan first goes into effect.

b. The insurer provides an administrative manual that explains how the plan operates.

c. If circumstances arise that are not covered by standard procedures, the insurer provides guidance or may handle the situation.

9. Lower.

10. • Is the employer capable of administering the plan?

• Does the employer prefer to reduce its premiums in exchange for relieving the insurer of administrative work, or does it prefer to pay the insurer more rather than take on these responsibilities?

11. Large.

12. Only a few.

13. a. External.

b. Internal.

c. Internal.

d. External.

e. External.

f. Internal.

14. • Are the employer's records accurate?

• Is the employer correctly following administrative procedures?

15. a. To make sure they are being completed properly.

b. To confirm the number of insured employees reported by the employer in the latest premium statement.

c. To verify that insured employees are eligible for coverage.

d. To determine if any claims were paid to employees who were not in fact covered by the policy.

16. Premium statements submitted by the employer.

17. They educate employer personnel on propel procedure so that fewer mistakes are made the future.

18. • Whether the insurer believes that the cost of auditing will be greater or less than the gains that result from it.

   • Whether state insurance department examiners require audits to protect the interests of those covered by the plans.

19. The employer.

20. An insurer.

21. Employer funds.

22. Insurer funds.

23. Coverage; administrative services.

24. Unusually high levels of claims.

25. The excess.

26. The insurer providing the coverage of the plan; the employer purchasing the coverage.

27. Staff; expertise.

28. Sometimes.

29. Both.

30. Neither Charley's Cheeses nor Shawnee wants the responsibility of administering the coverage.

31. Administrative services only; all administrative functions.

32. Claim services only; claims only.

33. Coverage.

34. Is not.

35. ERISA.

36. a. Self-insured plan with a third-party administrator.

   b. Fully insured, self-administered plan.

   c. Partially self-insured plan.

   d. Fully insured, insurer-administered plan.

   e. Self-insured plan with no third-party administrator.

2 THE ISSUANCE AND INSTALLATION OF POLICIES

Introduction (Page 7)

✦ 1. **Issuance**, narrowly defined, is the act whereby an insurance company officially _____ a policy to an applicant.

✦ 2. The term **issuance** is used more broadly to refer to _____.

✦ 3. **Installation** takes place in (an insurance company providing group coverage / a business purchasing group coverage).

Preissuance Activities for Group Policies (Pages 7–9)

4. In group insurance, preissuance activities involve working with employer personnel on three main tasks: _____, _____ and _____.

5. What preissuance activities does the insurer's group representative perform in connection with the application and the deposit?

6. Provisional enrollment of employees must take place as part of the group application process so that it can be determined whether _____ requirements have been met.

✦ 7. What are **minimum enrollment requirements**?

8. Announcement literature is prepared by (insurer / employer) personnel.

9. Announcement literature is usually distributed to employees by (insurer / employer) personnel.

11. Announcement literature includes four main pieces of information. What are they?

12. In addition to announcement literature, in what other way are employees informed about a health plan and encouraged to participate?

13. To enroll in a group plan, an employee must _____.

14. What information does an enrollment form typically include?

15. What purpose do enrollment forms serve in each of these areas?

   a. Minimum enrollment requirements.

   b. Underwriting.

   c. Plan administration.

   d. Employee choices.

   e. Payroll deductions.

15. In most cases, if an employee chooses not to enroll in a plan, he (simply does not fill out an enrollment card / is required to sign a waiver stating that he does not want to participate).

Issuance Activities for Group Policies (Pages 9–10)

16. An application for insurance is submitted to the _____ department, which determines whether the insurer will offer coverage and on what terms.

♦ 17. The information that will be needed to issue and administer a policy is consolidated into one document, called the _____.

♦ 18. What are some other terms used to refer to a case summary record?

♦ 19. The legal document that establishes the agreement between the insurer and the policyholder is known as the _____.

20. What does the master policy contain?

♦ 21. What is a **model policy**?

22. The provisions and wording of a model policy are adapted for two primary reasons. What are they?

♦ 23. A **certificate of insurance** is a document given (by the insurer to the employer / by the employer to the insured / by the insurer to the insured).

24. What kind of policy provisions does a certificate of insurance describe?

25. In group plans, a certificate of insurance (constitutes / does not constitute) a legal contract between the insurer and the employee.

26. In group plans, a contract (exists / does not exist) between the insurer and an employee.

♦ 27. What are the two common formats for certificates of insurance?

28. The (master policy / certificate-booklet) format uses less formal terminology.

29. The trend is toward the (master policy / certificate-booklet) format.

30. Insurers (are / are not) required by law to distribute identification cards to insured employees.

31. Identification cards provide evidence of _____ and information on how to _____.

32. What issuance tasks do insurer personnel perform in these areas?

    a. Billing.

    b. Forms.

    c. Manuals.

33. A group plan's administrative manual is designed primarily for the use of (insurer personnel / employer personnel / insureds).

Installation (Page 11)

♦ 34. **Installation** is the process by which an employer establishes the administrative procedures and structures necessary for _____.

35. Installation is handled by (insurer personnel / employer personnel / both).

♦ 36. A **plan administrator** is a member of the (employer's / insurer's) staff who is given the responsibility of managing a group insurance plan.

37. What do the insurer's group representative and the employer's plan administrator do in each of the following areas at their initial meeting?

   a. The policy.

   b. The administrative manual.

   c. Forms and other administrative materials.

   d. Record keeping.

   e. Claims.

   f. Certificates of insurance.

38. There is little standardization among insurance companies in the design or use of administrative forms except for (application / claim / billing) forms.

39. In some cases, some preissuance, issuance, and installation tasks normally performed by the insurer's group representative are handled by an agent or broker representing the insurer. This is most common for (small / large) groups.

Preissuance and Issuance of Individual Policies (Page 12)

40. For individual insurance, what are the four main preissuance activities?

41. In individual insurance, preissuance tasks are usually handled by an (agent or broker representing the insurer / insurer employee).

42. What difficulty does individual health insurance present in the area of issuance?

Answers

1. Offers.

2. Administrative activities associated with offering a new policy.

3. A business purchasing group coverage.

4. Completing and submitting the application, paying the deposit, and provisionally enrolling employees.

5. She obtains the application and the deposit from the employer, verifies that the application is complete and signed, and usually also completes a worksheet on the application with additional information needed for the underwriting and implementation of the policy.

6. Minimum enrollment.

7. Requirements that a minimal number or percentage of employees must enroll for the policy to be issued.

8. Insurer.

9. Employer.

10. • The benefits of the plan;

   • the requirements for eligibility to participate in the plan;

   • the amount of the employee contribution to premium; and

   • the proposed date on which the plan will go into effect.

11. Employee meetings.

12. Fill out, sign, and submit an enrollment form.

13. The employee's name, date of birth, sex, and occupation, as well as information on her dependents and (for some coverages) annual earnings.

14. a. Enrollment forms are the official record of how many employees have enrolled, and so they are the basis on which it is determined whether minimum enrollment requirements have been met.

   b. The employee information on the forms is used in underwriting.

   c. The forms provide information necessary for issuing certificates of coverage, for record keeping, and for other administrative tasks.

   d. The forms record employee choices, such as whether the employee wants dependent coverage or which coverage options the employee selects.

   e. The forms include employees' signed statements authorizing the employer to deduct their contributions to premiums from their wages.

15. He is required to sign a waiver stating that he does not want to participate.

16. Underwriting.

17. Case summary record.

18. Abstract, policy abstract, history card, specification sheet, and digest.

19. Master policy.

20. A statement that the insurer will provide coverage in return for premiums; the terms of the agreement, including who is eligible for benefits, under what circumstances benefits will be paid, the amount of benefits, and so forth.

21. A generic policy that is used in drawing up master policies.

22. The specifics of each case and the regulatory requirements of the state in which the policy will be in effect.

23. By the insurer to the insured.

24. Benefit provisions and other provisions that apply to the insureds.

25. Does not constitute.

26. Does not. (The contract exists between the insurer and the employer and is embodied in the master policy.)

27. The master policy format and the certificate-booklet format.

28. Certificate-booklet format.

29. Certificate-booklet format.

30. Are not.

31. Coverage; contact the insurer's customer service unit.

32. a. The billing department prepares the statement for a group's first premium.

b. Forms needed to administer the plan are prepared.

c. An administrative manual for the plan is prepared.

33. Employer personnel.

34. A new insurance plan to begin operating.

35. Both.

36. Employer's.

37. a. They review the provisions of the policy that pertain to administration.

b. The representative gives the administrator the administrative manual and reviews it with her.

c. The representative explains the purpose of each administrative form and how to complete it.

d. The representative and the administrator set up a system for maintaining insurance records for all covered employees.

e. The representative explains claim forms and acquaints the administrator with the deadlines and other requirements for filing claims.

f. The representative delivers the certificates of insurance. The representative and the administrator check the certificates for accuracy and make arrangements for their distribution to employees.

38. Claim.

39. Small.

40. Collecting the deposit; assisting the prospective policyholder in completing the application; reviewing the application for completeness and accuracy; and submitting the application and the deposit to the home office.

41. Agent or broker representing the insurer.

42. A great many different policies must be issued.

3 POLICY RENEWAL AND CHANGES

Introduction (Page 13)

✦ 1. An insurance policy is in effect for a stipulated period of time, called the _____ of the policy.

✦ 2. After this stipulated period expires, a policy may be continued. This continuation is called _____.

3. Typically, policies may be renewed (every six months for six months / every year for one year / every three years for three years).

4. Most commonly, changes are made in the coverage of a policy (at renewal / at any time).

5. Changes are commonly made in the persons covered by a policy (at renewal / at any time).

Renewal or Nonrenewal? (Page 14)

6. An insurer (always has / usually has / usually does not have / never has) the right to decline to renew a health insurance policy.

7. With a few exceptions, HIPAA requires insurers to renew (group / individual / both group and individual) policies providing (medical expense coverage only / disability income coverage only / any kind of health coverage).

8. For health coverages other than medical expense insurance, regulations (always / sometimes / never) permit an insurer to nonrenew a policy.

9. Renewal provisions that permit insurers to nonrenew only under certain limited circumstances are most typical of (group / individual) health insurance policies.

10. Some companies nonrenew only under specific circumstances. What are the four most common of these circumstances?

✦ 11. An insured known to engage in dishonest or dangerous behavior is considered a _____

Changes in Coverage (Pages 14–16)

12. If an insurer is losing money or fears it may lose money on a policy, it most commonly (nonrenews / proposes an increase in premium or a change in coverage as a condition of renewal).

13. Generally, when an insurer proposes changes as a condition of renewal, which of these options does the policyholder have? Renewing the policy with the proposed changes / renewing the policy without the proposed changes / not renewing the policy.

14. The changes in a policy that an insurer can propose at renewal are (always / sometimes / never) limited by regulations or the renewal provisions of the policy.

15. Changes to a policy at renewal may be proposed by (the insurer only / the policyholder only / either or both).

♦ 16. An **increase in coverage** is any change in a policy that _____.

♦ 17. A **decrease in coverage** is any change in a policy that _____.

18. Is each of the following an increase or a decrease in coverage?

   a. Adding a new benefit.

   b. Eliminating an existing benefit.

   c. Increasing the amount of an existing benefit.

   d. Reducing the amount of a benefit.

   e. Increasing deductibles or coinsurance.

   f. Decreasing deductibles or coinsurance.

19. An increase in coverage is associated with (higher / lower) premiums.

20. In recent years a particular type of decrease in coverage has commonly been used to hold down premium increases caused by the rising cost of health care. What type of decrease is this?

The Renewal Process (Pages 16–17)

21. Renewal underwriting differs from initial underwriting primarily in that underwriters must look for and take into account three things. What are they?

22. What changes in circumstances at renewal are most important for group plans?

23. What changes in circumstances are most important for individual policies?

24. Stansfield Electric has a group plan with Abacus Insurance. Recently Abacus's administrative costs for Stansfield's plan have been driven up by many small claims. What can Abacus do at renewal?

25. Insurer personnel have most of the information they need for renewal underwriting for which of these? Insurer-administered group plans / self-administered group plans / individual policies.

RENEWAL AND CHANGES ♦ *13*

26. An individual policyholder may have to submit a new application with an updated medical history at renewal if she requests (an increase in coverage / a decrease in coverage / either).

27. Renewal underwriting results in an insurer deciding on one of the following options: renewal with no change / renewal with a change / nonrenewal. Which one is least common?

28. Sometimes an insurer will offer two alternatives at renewal. What are the most common alternatives?

29. Most states require that the insurer notify the policyholder of its renewal decision in writing at least (30 / 60 / 90) days before the decision is to go into effect.

30. Usually, a renewal notice is sent to (the policyholder only / the agent or group sales representative working with the policyholder only / both).

Implementing Changes in Coverage (Pages 17–18)

31. When changes are made in a policy or a new coverage is added, (a new master policy must be issued / a rider may be added to the existing master policy / either, depending on the case).

32. If there is a choice, insurers prefer (adding a rider to an existing policy / issuing a new policy).

33. For group policies, what documents and materials may have to be prepared or revised at renewal?

34. Under what two circumstances may enrollment be necessary when a group plan is renewed?

35. When changes are made in a policy or a new coverage is added, (new certificates of insurance must be issued / riders may be added to the existing certificates / either, depending on the case).

Changes in Group Plan Enrollment (Pages 18–20)

36. Most commonly, new employees become eligible for coverage under a group plan (immediately upon hiring / after a probationary waiting period).

37. The duration of probationary waiting periods is usually (one to three months / three to six months / six months to a year).

38. If a plan is (contributory / noncontributory), employees automatically become insured when they become eligible.

39. If a plan is (contributory / noncontributory), employees begin receiving coverage as soon as they both become eligible and choose to participate.

40. In most group plans, a new employee will be automatically accepted if she joins no later than (10 / 31 / 90) days after the date she becomes eligible.

♦ 41. An employee who does not join a group plan within a certain time after he becomes eligible and then decides to join later is called a _____.

♦ 42. Health information and other information that an applicant for insurance provides to prove that she is an acceptable insurance risk is known as _____.

♦ 43. A period, usually lasting a few weeks and occurring once a year, during which employees can add or change coverage is known as an _____.

44. To join a group plan, a late entrant must (provide evidence of insurability / wait until the next open enrollment period / either, depending on the plan).

45. Certificates of insurance are issued to all newly insured employees by (all / most / some) insurers.

♦ 46. The page of a certificate of insurance that names the insured and states that she has the coverage described in the certificate is called the _____ page or the _____ page.

47. Insurers use three common alternatives to issuing certificates of insurance to all newly insured employees. Describe each of these.

48. Usually, an employee leaves a group plan for one of three reasons. What are they?

49. When an employee leaves a group plan because she is no longer eligible, the employer must report three items of information to the insurer. What are they?

50. To voluntarily withdraw from a group plan an employee normally must _____.

51. When an employee voluntarily withdraws from a group plan, her dependents (can / cannot) continue coverage.

52. There are two reasons why dependent coverage may begin or end for an employee. What are they?

53. To add dependent coverage an employee must normally _____.

54. If after dependent coverage has begun an employee wants to add an additional dependent, (he may have to apply for coverage / coverage always is granted automatically).

55. If a child is born to an employee with dependent coverage, (the child automatically receives coverage and no employee action is required / the employee must usually apply for coverage for the child / the child automatically receives coverage but the employee must notify the insurer).

Changes in Insureds in Individual Policies (Pages 20–21)

56. The handling of changes in dependent coverage for individual policies differs from that of group plans in two ways. What are they?

57. Some individual policies include a conversion privilege for dependent children reaching adulthood. What is required by this privilege?

Answers

1. Term.

2. Renewal.

3. Every year for one year.

4. At renewal.

5. At any time.

6. Usually does not have.

7. Both group and individual; medical expense coverage only.

8. Sometimes.

9. Individual.

10. • The insured has engaged in fraud.

    • The insured is considered a moral hazard.

    • The insured is overinsured.

    • The insurer is nonrenewing an entire class of policies.

11. Moral hazard.

12. Proposes an increase in premium or a change in coverage as a condition of renewal.

13. Renewing the policy with the proposed changes or not renewing the policy.

14. Sometimes.

15. Either or both.

16. Increases the amount of money the insurance company is likely to have to pay in benefits.

17. Reduces the amount the insurer will likely pay in benefits.

18. a. Increase.

    b. Decrease.

    c. Increase.

    d. Decrease.

    e. Decrease.

    f. Increase.

19. Higher.

20. Higher deductibles.

21. • Any changes in the circumstances of the policyholder or insureds;

    • any problems connected with the policy; and

    • any changes in coverage requested by the policyholder.

22. Changes in the financial status of the employer, the size of the group, the characteristics of the group (such as age or gender composition), or the proportion of employees who participate in the plan.

23. Changes in the policyholder's age, occupation, or income.

24. Propose an increase in deductibles or longer elimination periods.

25. Insurer-administered group plans and individual policies.

26. An increase in coverage.

27. Nonrenewal.

28. No change in coverage but an increase in premium; or a decrease in coverage and no increase in premium or a smaller increase.

29. 30 days.

30. Both.

31. Either, depending on the case.

32. Adding a rider to an existing policy.

33. The master policy, the certificates of insurance, announcement literature, the administrative manual, premium statements, and other forms and administrative materials.

34. When additional employees are made eligible for coverage and when employees already enrolled in the plan receive a new coverage.

35. Either, depending on the case.

36. After a probationary waiting period.

37. One to three months.

38. Noncontributory.

39. Contributory.

40. 31 days.

41. Late entrant.

42. Evidence of insurability.

43. Open enrollment period.

44. Either, depending on the plan.

45. Some.

46. The validation page or the face page.

47. • The insurer provides the policyholder with a supply of certificates with no validation page. When an employee is added to the plan, the insurer completes a validation page with the employee's name and sends it to the policyholder. The policyholder attaches the validation page to a certificate and delivers it to the employee.

• As above, the policyholder keeps a supply of certificates with no validation page. When an employee joins the group, the policyholder affixes a sticker with the validation information to a certificate and delivers it to the employee.

• Employees receive no certificates with personalized validation. Instead they receive booklets that indicate that they are insured if they meet the conditions set forth in the booklet.

48. • The employee ceases to be employed by the group policyholder.

• The employee remains employed by the policyholder but changes jobs so that she is no longer in a class of employees covered by the plan.

• The employee voluntarily chooses to stop participating in a contributory plan.

49. The employee's name, the exact date of her termination of eligibility, and the reason for the termination.

50. Sign a statement saying that he no longer authorizes his employer to deduct premium contributions from his paycheck.

51. Cannot.

52. • An employee may have dependents at times and not at other times.

• In a contributory plan, an employee may choose to add or drop dependent coverage.

53. Sign a form that authorizes increased payroll deductions.

54. He may have to apply for coverage.

55. The child automatically receives coverage but the employee must notify the insurer.

56. • When a new dependent is added to an individual policy, a rider must sometimes be issued and attached to the policy.

• When a child is no longer eligible for dependent coverage under an individual policy because he has reached the maximum age or married, the insurer usually tries to continue coverage by selling the child his own policy.

57. The insurer must provide individual coverage to the adult child if he does not have coverage through employment, marriage, or some other source.

4 PREMIUM BILLING AND PAYMENT

The Premium Statement (Pages 23–26)

◆ 1. A **premium statement** is a notice that _____.

2. Group policyholders know (when premiums are due only / the amount of premium due only / both).

3. Individual policyholders know (when premiums are due only / the amount of premium due only / both).

4. The amount of group premium for each billing period usually depends on the number of _____.

5. Why does the number of persons covered by a group policy change from billing period to billing period?

6. Normally, the amount of the premium of an individual policy (is the same every time / varies from billing period to billing period).

7. Insurers normally send premium statements on a regular basis to (individual policyholders only / group policyholders only / both).

8. For an individual policy, an insurer generally (has / does not have) a contractual obligation to send a premium statement.

9. Why do insurers send premium statements to individual policyholders?

10. In self-administered group plans, the amount of premium due is usually calculated by the (insurer / policyholder).

11. In self-administered group plans, insurers usually verify that they are receiving the correct premium amounts by (preparing their own monthly premium statements / auditing the policyholder / both).

12. Generally, group policies have (monthly premiums / quarterly premiums / annual premiums / a variety of premium schedules).

13. Generally, individual policies have (monthly premiums / quarterly premiums / annual premiums / a variety of premium schedules).

◆ 14. In group insurance, the **premium rate** is normally (the regular total amount of premium / the amount of premium per insured).

15. In group insurance, the policyholder and the insurer agree on a (premium amount / premium rate).

16. Explain how each of these criteria can be used to assign different premium rates to different members of an insured group.

    a. Coverages.

    b. Dependent coverage.

    c. Classes.

    d. Age bands.

17. In group insurance, the premium amount for any billing period is obtained by multiplying _____ by _____.

♦ 18. Described below are three ways in which a group premium statement can report and bill for the number of insureds at each rate. Name each.

    a. The premium statement lists every employee insured during the current month and the premium rate for each.

    b. The statement lists only those employees whose coverage status or rate has changed during the month.

    c. A premium amount is computed at the beginning of each year, based on the number of insureds charged each rate at that time, and the policyholder pays this amount on each premium due date during the year.

19. In most cases the total amount of premiums paid for the year with level billing is very close to the amount that would have been paid with list or exception billing. How does this happen?

20. The most common billing method for smaller groups is (list billing / exception billing / level billing).

21. Exception billing is used most often with (small / large) groups.

22. Level billing is becoming (more / less) common.

23. Level billing works best with groups that experience little _____.

24. Gilbert Swann is hired by the Tansonville Company on August 21, and immediately becomes covered by Tansonville's group health plan. Tansonville's group premium is due on the first day of every month. When Tansonville pays its September 1 premium, Gilbert has been covered for 10 days. What amount will Tansonville pay for Gilbert? (A full amount, as if he had been covered for a whole month / nothing, as if he had not been covered for any part of the month / one third of the full amount, reflecting his part-month coverage).

25. Albert Angostini leaves the employment of the Tansonville Company on September 15 and is covered by Tansonville's group plan up to that date. Thus Albert was covered for 15 days of the month. In its October 1 premium payment, what amount will Tansonville pay for Albert? (A full amount, as if he had been covered for a whole month / nothing, as if he had not been covered for any part of the month / one half of the full amount, reflecting his part-month coverage).

26. For an individual who is covered as of the premium due date but was not covered for the entire month, most group policies charge (the full monthly premium amount / nothing / a prorated premium amount).

27. For an individual who is *not* covered as of the premium due date but *was* covered for part of the month, most group policies charge (the full monthly premium amount / nothing / a prorated premium amount).

28. Why do both insurers and employers accept the above rules?

29. In (all / some / no) group and individual policies, insureds may make changes in coverage in the middle of a billing period.

30. The date on which the premium statement is prepared is called the _____ date or the _____ date.

31. Normally, a premium statement is based on coverage as of the (premium due date / billing date / annual date).

32. The billing date is usually about (3 / 10 / 30) days before the premium due date.

33. In order for a change in coverage to be reflected in a new premium statement, the change must be requested (by the premium due date / by the billing date / several days before the billing date).

34. Charles Barron has an individual health insurance policy. He requests a change in coverage that will reduce his premium. However, he requests the change too late for it to be reflected in his next quarterly premium statement. Probably, his insurer will (not make the change in coverage until the following quarter / make the change in coverage now but not change the premium amount until the following quarter / make the changes in coverage and premium now, but require Charles to pay the former amount on this quarter's bill and be credited for his overpayment later).

Group Billing and Payment (Pages 26–27)

35. What is the traditional method of group premium payment?

36. A post office box held by an insurer that a bank has access to is known as a _____.

37. How does a lock box work?

38. What are the two advantages of the lock-box arrangement?

39. How do **preauthorized checks** (PACs) work in the payment of premiums?

40. Preauthorized checks are most common with (small / large) groups.

41. Persistency is better with the (PAC / traditional) approach to premium payment.

42. The electronic movement of money from the policyholder's account to the insurer's is known as _____.

43. EFT can be (a variation on the traditional payment method / used with the PAC method / either).

44. What two advantages does EFT offer group policyholders?

Individual Billing and Payment (Pages 27–29)

♦ 45. In the individual insurance field, the traditional method of premium payment, whereby the policyholder mails a check to the insurer in response to a regular premium statement, is known as _____.

46. In individual insurance, there are two problems with the traditional billing and payment system. What are they?

47. Insurers address the high cost of frequent payment schedules by (offering only less frequent payment schedules / offering a choice of schedules, but charging more for more frequent schedules / either).

48. Higher charges for more frequent payment schedules serve two purposes. What are they?

♦ 49. Which two of these methods of payment does the term **automatic bank payments** refer to? The lock-box method / preauthorized checks / electronic funds transfer.

50. Automatic bank payments have the same advantages for individual insurance as they do for group insurance—a reduction in administrative costs and an improvement in cash flow. But in individual insurance they have an additional advantage. What is it?

51. With automatic bank payments, how is payment confirmed?

52. The increase in credit card payment of premiums has been motivated by (consumers / insurers).

53. What is the advantage to insurers of charging premiums to policyholders' credit cards?

54. What is the disadvantage to insurers of charging premiums to policyholders' credit cards?

55. With credit card payment, how is payment confirmed?

♦ 56. In a **franchise plan**, an insurer sells (a group policy to an employer for its employees / a group policy to employees of a business acting collectively / individual policies to employees of a business).

57. In a franchise plan, the policyholder is the (employer / group / individual).

58. In a franchise plan, the insurer submits a bill to and receives payment from the (employer / group / individual).

59. In franchise plans, payment (is always by the traditional remittance method / can be by payroll deduction).

The Grace Period, Termination, and Reinstatement (Page 29)

60. During the grace period for payment of premiums, if the policyholder fails to pay a premium, the insurer (may / may not) terminate the policy.

61. If the grace period for payment of premiums expires and the premium is still not paid, coverage (ceases / continues for another 10 days / continues until the insurer formally terminates the policy).

62. If the grace period for payment of premiums expires and the premium is still not paid, the insurer (may / may not) terminate the policy.

63. If the grace period for payment of premiums expires and the premium is still not paid, an insurer usually (terminates the policy immediately / tries to persuade the policyholder to pay the premium and continue the policy).

64. The grace period begins on the (billing date / premium due date / renewal date) and most commonly lasts (10 / 31 / 60) days.

65. The grace period is intended to protect the (policyholder / insurer).

66. Regulations require (all / most / some) individual health insurance policies to have a grace period for the payment of premiums.

67. (All / Most / Some) group policies have a grace period for payment of premiums.

♦ 68. A policyholder does not pay a premium and the policy is terminated. Later, the policyholder pays the overdue premium and the insurer puts the policy back into effect. This is known as _____.

69. Individual policyholders (always / sometimes / never) have to apply for reinstatement.

70. Odette Crecy has an individual health insurance policy with Balbec Insurance. She fails to pay a premium, the grace period expires, and Balbec terminates the policy. Later, Odette requests reinstatement of the policy and submits payment of the premium. Balbec accepts the payment without requiring Odette to submit an application with it. If Odette's policy is typical, Balbec (can request an application any time during the following year / has 45 days to request an application / must reinstate the policy without an application).

71. Suppose in the above example, Balbec required that Odette submit an application for reinstatement with her late premium payment. Thirty days after receiving the payment, Balbec still has not notified Odette whether it will reinstate the policy. Balbec (must reinstate the policy / may not reinstate the policy / has 15 more days to decide).

72. If Balbec has not notified Odette of its decision two months after receiving the late payment, it (must reinstate the policy / may not reinstate the policy / can reinstate the policy or not as it wishes).

Summary (Page 30)

73. In (group / individual) insurance, preparing each statement is usually not complicated, but there are a great many statements.

74. In (group / individual) insurance, there are a small number of statements, but for each one the amount of premium must be calculated.

Answers

1. A premium of a certain amount is due by a certain date.

2. When premiums are due only.

3. Both.

4. People covered by the policy during that period.

5. Employees come and go, choose to receive coverage or give up coverage, add or drop dependent coverage, or join a different class of employee with different coverage.

6. Is the same every time.

7. Both.

8. Does not have.

9. If they did not, the collection of premiums would be irregular and many policies would lapse due to nonpayment.

10. Policyholder.

11. Auditing the policyholder.

12. Monthly premiums.

13. A variety of premium schedules.

14. The amount of premium per insured.

15. Premium rate.

16. a. Members who receive different coverages are charged different rates.

    b. Members who have coverage for their dependents and those who do not are charged different rates.

    c. Members in different occupational classes are charged different rates.

    d. Members in different age groups are charged different rates.

17. Each premium rate by the number of people who were insured at that rate during the period.

18. a. List billing.

    b. Exception billing.

    c. Level or equal installment billing.

19. The number of people beginning and ending coverage and changing rate categories balance out over the course of the year.

20. List billing.

21. Large.

22. Less.

23. Turnover and fluctuations in size.

24. A full amount.

25. Nothing.

26. The full monthly premium amount.

27. Nothing.

28. Because in the long term overpayments and underpayments balance out and both parties benefit from the simplification of billing.

29. Some.

30. Billing date or billing calculation date.

31. Billing date.

32. 10 days.

33. Several days before the billing date.

34. Make the changes in coverage and premium now, but require Charles to pay the former amount on this quarter's bill and be credited for his overpayment later.

35. An insurer sends a premium statement to a group policyholder, the policyholder mails its payment in the form of a check to the insurer, and the insurer deposits the check at its bank.

36. Lock box.

37. Policyholders mail premium payments to the lock box and the bank collects payments on a daily basis and deposits them in the insurer's account.

38. • The money paid is deposited in the insurer's account more quickly and can begin earning interest or be available for insurer use or investment.

• Insurer administrative personnel do not have to receive, endorse, and deposit payment checks.

39. Policyholders give the insurer preauthorized checks for payment of premiums. Each month the insurer sends the policyholder a premium statement showing the amount the insurer will draw from the policyholder's account by means of a preauthorized check.

40. Small.

41. PAC.

42. Electronic funds transfer (EFT).

43. Either.

44. The elimination of the administrative work of issuing and mailing checks and an improvement in cash flow.

45. Direct billing.

46. • High administrative costs (due to the very large number of statements and payments that must be prepared and received); and

• a high incidence of nonpayment and lapses of policies for nonpayment.

47. Either.

48. To cover the higher costs of frequent schedules and to discourage their use.

49. Preauthorized checks and electronic funds transfer.

50. The insurer does not send premium statements.

51. In the policyholder's bank statement.

52. Consumers.

53. Premium statements do not have to be sent.

54. They must pay a fee to the credit card company.

55. In the policyholder's credit card bill.

56. Individual policies to employees of a business.

57. Individual.

58. Employer.

59. Can be by payroll deduction.

60. May not.

61. Ceases.

62. May.

63. Tries to persuade the policyholder to pay the premium and continue the policy.

64. Premium due date; 31 days.

65. Policyholder.

66. All.

67. Most.

68. Reinstatement.

69. Sometimes.

70. Must reinstate the policy without an application.

71. Has 15 more days to decide.

72. Must reinstate the policy.

73. Individual.

74. Group.

5 CLAIM ADMINISTRATION

Introduction (Page 31)

✦ 1. Another set of terms is increasingly used in place of "claims," "claim administration," and "claim department." These terms are _____, _____, and _____.

Home Office Claim Departments (Pages 31–32)

2. What three main advantages does an insurer gain by handling all claim administration in its home office instead of in several field claim offices?

✦ 3. Serenity Insurance Company sells medical expense insurance, disability income insurance, and several supplemental coverages. The company is divided into major departments for sales, marketing, underwriting, claims, and other areas. Each of these departments works with all the coverages Serenity sells. Thus, the claim department handles claims for all types of coverage. This type of claim administration organization is called _____.

✦ 4. Tranquility Insurance Company sells the same coverages as Serenity. It is divided into major departments for each type of coverage. These major departments are divided into smaller departments, each of which handles an area of activity associated with that coverage, such as sales, marketing, underwriting, and claims. Thus, there is a separate claim department for each coverage. This type of claim administration organization is called _____.

5. Which does each of these statements describe, single department organization or product line organization?

   a. Departmental procedures and policies can be tailored to one coverage.

   b. Specialization in departmental procedures and policies is limited.

   c. Departmental personnel can become very experienced in the particular needs and problems of one coverage.

   d. Departmental personnel can become somewhat experienced in one coverage, but must be able to handle several coverages.

   e. There is a high degree of consistency in the treatment of claims for the insurer's different types of coverage.

   f. There may be a lack of consistency in the treatment of claims for the insurer's different types of coverage.

Field Claim Offices (Pages 32–33)

♦ 6. An organizational approach in which claim administration takes place in several field claim offices is known as _____.

7. How can maintaining several field claim offices enable an insurer to provide better service?

8. The number of field claim offices that an insurer maintains depends on three main factors. What are they?

9. The current trend is toward (one central claim office / several field claim offices).

Self-Administration (Pages 33–34)

10. In self-administered group plans, claim administration is handled by (the employer / the insurer / either or both).

11. Insurers most commonly let employers handle claims for coverages that are relatively _____.

♦ 12. Some employers receive claims from their employees, review them to verify coverage, and submit them to the insurer for processing and payment. This is known as _____.

13. The more common practice is (employer claim administration / policyholder submission).

14. When the employer handles claims in a self-administered group plan, the insurer is involved with the employer's claim personnel in three main ways. What are they?

♦ 15. Give the name of each of these types of claim audits:

   a. Any claim in excess of a certain amount is referred to insurer personnel for review and approval before payment is made.

   b. The employer's plan administrator sends the insurer a random sample of claim files of cases that have been closed. Insurer claim personnel review the cases to determine whether proper procedures were followed.

   c. A representative of the insurer visits the employer and reviews randomly selected closed and active files to determine whether proper procedures are being followed.

16. The most common method by which insurers reimburse employers for claim payments is the _____ system.

17. When a draft on an account is submitted, (there must be / there do not have to be) sufficient funds in the account.

18. In the draft book system, when an employer pays a claim, it submits a draft on the account of the insurer. The insurer (must accept and pay the draft / only accepts the draft if it approves the claim).

Answers

1. "Benefits," "benefits administration," and "benefits department."

2. • It is usually less costly to maintain one large unit rather than several smaller ones.

   • Training is centralized and communication simplified, making it easier to maintain consistent and correct practices.

   • All claim personnel are in close proximity to other insurer staff they may need to consult, such as physicians and attorneys.

3. Single department organization.

4. Product line organization.

5. a. Product line organization.

   b. Single department organization.

   c. Product line organization.

   d. Single department organization.

   e. Single department organization.

   f. Product line organization.

6. Geographic organization.

7. It can provide more personalized service.

8. The geographic distribution of its policyholders and insured population; the type of coverages it offers; and the number of field offices maintained by its competitors.

9. One central claim office.

10. Either or both.

11. Uncomplicated.

12. Policyholder submission.

13. Policyholder submission.

14. • Insurer personnel usually assist in the training of employer claim personnel.

    • Many insurers require employer personnel to consult with insurer claim staff when they deal with a complicated or questionable claim.

    • Insurers conduct periodic audits of the claim operations of employers to ensure that the appropriate procedures are in place and are being followed.

15. a. Large amount audit.

    b. Random sample audit.

    c. On-site audit.

16. Policyholder draft (or draft book) system.

17. There do not have to be.

18. Only accepts the draft if it approves the claim.

6 THE SUBMISSION OF CLAIMS

Introduction (Page 35)

✦ 1. An **insurance claim** is a statement that _____ accompanied by _____.

Direct Submission (Pages 35–36)

✦ 2. In **direct submission** of claims, insureds submit claims to their (employer / insurer).

3. Describe the two ways in which direct submission has traditionally operated.

✦ 4. Bill Tolson makes a formal request to his insurer that the insurer pay benefits directly to his physician. Bill is _____ benefits.

5. The card-only approach and the claim-kit approach to submission of claims were originally created for (large group plans / small group plans / individual policies).

6. The card-only approach is a variation on (insured / provider) submission of claims.

7. How does the card-only approach work?

8. In the card-only approach, what information is on the insured's identification card?

9. What is included in a claim kit?

10. In the claim-kit system, for (major / minor) services the insured uses the card-only approach.

11. In the claim-kit system, for (major / minor) services the insured pays the provider out of her own pocket and submits a claim to the insurer.

12. The (card-only / claim-kit) system is much more common.

Self-Administered Plans and Policyholder Submission (Pages 36–37)

✦ 13. In some group plans, employees submit claims to their employer, which submits them to the insurer. This practice is known as _____.

14. In policyholder submission, the main function of the employer in the claim process is to confirm that _____.

15. In policyholder submission, the insurer pays benefits (directly to the insured or a provider / to the employer, which passes the payment to the insured / either).

16. In policyholder submission, the employer (must / need not) maintain an insurance record for each covered employee.

17. The more common practice is (policyholder submission / direct submission).

18. Policyholder submission is most common among (small and medium-size employers / large employers).

The Two Steps in Submitting a Claim (Pages 37–38)

19. The two steps in submitting a claim are submitting _____ and submitting _____.

20. In a notice of claim, the insured or a provider notifies the insurer that _____.

21. What two main purposes does notice of claim serve?

22. A notice of claim provision is contained in (all / most / some) group and individual health insurance policies.

23. Typically a notice of claim must be made in writing within (20 / 60 / 90) days after the loss or as soon thereafter as is reasonably possible.

24. How do insureds usually provide proof of loss?

25. Providers provide proof of loss by submitting (insurer claim forms / their own claim forms / a bill / any of these).

26. Most insurers will accept (only their own claim forms / any form or bill with the necessary information).

27. Alice Marvel has incurred a covered loss and already has the appropriate insurer claim form. Can she simply complete and submit the claim form and have it serve as both notice of claim and proof of loss?

28. Contract provisions typically state that proof of loss must be submitted within (20 / 60 / 90) days after the loss or as soon as is reasonably possible.

29. Standardized claim forms are intended to make the claim process more _____ and therefore less complicated and easier.

♦ 30. Which standardized claim form(s) is described?

   a. It is used by hospitals and other institutions.

   b. It is used by physicians and other noninstitutional health care providers.

   c. It provides information on diagnoses, treatments, services, supplies, and charges.

Answers

1. A covered loss has occurred; information about the loss and sometimes proof of it.

2. Insurer.

3. • An insured receives health care services, fills out a claim form, and sends the form, along with any necessary information and documentation, to the insurer. If the claim is valid, the insurer pays the benefit to the insured, who then pays the health care provider if she has not already done so. Alternatively, the insurer pays the benefit directly to the provider.

   • The provider, with the authorization of the insured, fills out a claim form and submits it along with a bill on the insured's behalf. The insurer pays the benefit directly to the provider.

4. Assigning.

5. Large group plans.

6. Provider.

7. When the insured needs health care services, she presents her identification card to the provider, who submits the claim and is paid by the insurer.

8. The card states that the cardholder has health coverage, summarizes the benefits she is entitled to, and indicates that the insurer will pay these benefits directly to the health care provider.

9. An identification card like that used in the card-only system, plus claim forms and instructions on how to submit a claim.

10. Major.

11. Minor.

12. Card-only.

13. Policyholder submission.

14. The employee has coverage.

15. Either.

16. Must.

17. Direct submission.

18. Small and medium-size employers.

19. Notice of claim; proof of loss.

20. A loss covered by the policy has occurred.

21. • It makes the insurer aware that it should begin the preliminary work of assembling a claim file and determining the status of the policy.

    • It serves as a request by the insured for forms needed for submitting proof of loss.

22. All.

23. 20 days.

24. By answering the questions on a claim form supplied by the insurer and attaching any bills or other documentation to it.

25. Any of these.

26. Any form or bill with the necessary information.

27. Yes, provided she can submit the form within the deadline for notice of claim. If she cannot meet this deadline, she must first submit notice of claim and later submit proof of loss.

28. 90 days.

29. Uniform.

30. a. The Uniform Billing Form (UB-92; HCFA-1450).

    b. The Health Insurance Claim Form (HCFA-1500)

    c. Both the Uniform Billing Form and the Health Insurance Claim Form.

7 CLAIM PROCESSING

Introduction (Page 43)

1. The two principal determinations made in claim processing are whether _____ and, if so, what _____.

2. To make these determinations, claim personnel examine the _____ and the _____,

3. There are two main reasons why examining and processing health insurance claims is complicated. What are they?

4. Claim processing essentially consists of seeking the answers to three questions. What are they?

Was Coverage in Effect? (Pages 44–46)

✦ 5. In claim processing, the first issue that must be addressed is whether the claimant was in fact covered by the policy when the loss occurred. This issue is known as _____.

6. What three questions must be answered to determine status of coverage?

7. For a group plan, the issue of status of coverage must be addressed on the _____ and _____ levels.

8. In a group plan, both _____ and _____ must be in effect at the time of loss or the insurer is not liable for benefits.

9. In policyholder submission, the group policyholder is responsible for _____ before submitting a claim to the insurer.

10. The date of a loss is not always easy to establish because in many cases it is difficult to precisely determine when _____.

11. For practical purposes, the date of the onset of a medical condition is defined as the date when (the first symptoms appeared / medical treatment was first sought / diagnosis was made).

12. In July, Paul Johnson began to experience symptoms of asthma. Despite his discomfort and the danger the symptoms posed, he did not consult a physician until October. Paul's medical condition is considered to have begun in (July / October). Why?

✦ 13. The date on which an insured begins to be covered by an insurance policy is known as the _____.

14. In (group / individual / both group and individual) policies, a specific calendar date is established as the effective date.

15. In (group / individual / both group and individual) policies, it is usually stipulated that the effective date is the date of application.

16. What conditions must be met for coverage to go into effect on the date of application?

17. During the grace period, coverage remains in effect for (individual policies only / group policies only / both individual and group policies).

18. Losses incurred during the grace period are covered (only if the policy is eventually reinstated / only if the policy is not reinstated / whether the policy is reinstated or not).

19. For (individual policies only / group policies only / both individual and group policies), if a policy lapses and is not reinstated, coverage does not continue after the end of the grace period.

20. For (individual policies only / group policies only / both individual and group policies), if a policy lapses and is reinstated, losses incurred after the end of the grace period but before reinstatement are covered.

21. Most states require that when individual policies are reinstated, coverage must be provided for injuries that occur (after the end of the grace period and before reinstatement / after the date of reinstatement / more than 10 days after the date of reinstatement).

22. Most states require that when individual policies are reinstated, coverage must be provided for illnesses that begin (after the end of the grace period and before reinstatement / after the date of reinstatement / more than 10 days after the date of reinstatement).

23. The most common reason that a policy is invalid is that the policyholder _____.

♦ 24. What is a **misrepresentation**?

♦ 25. A **material misrepresentation** is a false statement significant enough that if the insurer had known the truth, it would have _____ or would have _____.

26. The most common instance of a material misrepresentation is when an applicant for individual coverage does not report _____.

27. If a material misrepresentation is such that the insurer would not have offered coverage under any circumstances, the insurer usually _____ the policy.

28. If a material misrepresentation is such that the insurer would have offered a policy with a special provision, the insurer may offer to _____.

♦ 29. An insurer is permitted to rescind an individual insurance policy because of misrepresentations in the application only during a certain period of time following the issue date of the policy. This period is known as the _____. Depending on the state, this period lasts (six or nine months / two or three years / three or five years).

Is the Loss Covered? (Pages 46–47)

30. Once it has been established that the claimant's coverage was in effect at the time of the loss, claim examiners look at the claim form, bills, and other documents and ask three questions. What are they?

31. What are a claim examiner's first steps in determining if a loss is covered?

32. Next, the examiner determines whether the type of expense claimed is covered by the _____ provisions of the policy.

33. Policy provisions that sometimes disallow expenses otherwise covered by the benefit provisions include provisions for _____, _____, _____, and _____.

♦ 34. **Screening guides** are used to screen for services that _____.

35. For various medical conditions, screening guides contain information on _____, _____, and _____.

36. The information in screening guides are obtained from _____, _____, and _____.

What Is the Amount of Benefit? (Pages 47–50)

37. In some cases the dollar amount of a benefit is set by the policy. Two examples are _____ and _____.

38. A benefit schedule determines benefit amounts by setting _____.

♦ 39. When **eligible charge** limits are used, the benefit amount for a service is _____, as long as _____.

♦ 40. A **reasonable and customary charge** for a service is the amount _____.

41. The eligible charge limit for a service (is defined as the reasonable and customary charge for that service / is defined as the reasonable and customary charge or the provider's usual charge, whichever is less / may be defined in either way, depending on the policy).

42. If a provider charges more than the eligible charge limit of a policy, normally the insurer pays (the amount charged by the provider / the amount of the eligible charge limit / an amount between the provider's charge and the eligible charge limit).

43. Guidelines for reasonable and customary charges are established (nationally by the Prevailing Healthcare Charges. System / by each state insurance department for that state / by each insurance company for that company).

44. Different insurers arrive at somewhat different reasonable and customary charge amounts because they may use different _____ and somewhat different _____.

45. The Prevailing Healthcare Charges System (PHCS) obtains information on the amounts charged for various health care services primarily from (insurers / providers / government agencies).

46. PHCS disseminates information on health care charges primarily through (the media / reports made available to all interested parties as a public service / reports sent to insurers who subscribe to the service).

47. PHCS provides information on health care charges by (service only / service and geographic area).

48. Insurers who receive information from PHCS generally (rely entirely or largely on PHCS data / combine PHCS data with their own claim data) in setting their reasonable and customary charge amounts.

49. After the claim examiner has calculated the amount of a benefit based on a preset amount, a benefit schedule, or the provider's charges and eligible charge limits, she must consider two additional factors before she can determine the amount of benefit payment. What are they?

♦ 50. Sometimes a single loss is covered by two different insurance policies. This phenomenon is known as _____.

51. Describe four ways in which overinsurance can occur in the health insurance field.

52. Overinsurance drives up the cost of insurance in two ways. What are they?

♦ 53. **Coordination of benefits (COB)** is a process whereby two or more insurance companies that insure the same person for the same losses coordinate their payments of benefits so that they do not _____.

54. COB is used to make sure that the amount of benefits received by an insured is never greater than _____.

55. COB is used (for group policies only / for individual policies only / primarily for group policies but also for some individual policies / primarily for individual policies but also for some group policies / for group and individual policies equally).

56. To implement COB, claim examiners identify _____ and apply rules that divide _____.

57. Felicity Insurance Company issues a policy with a COB provision. The purpose of this provision is to stipulate, in the case when a loss is also covered by another policy, what _____.

58. COB provisions of different policies vary, but there is a considerable degree of uniformity, as most policies follow the guidelines of _____.

59. Under COB, the primary policy pays, _____ and the secondary policy pays additional benefits.

60. According to NAIC guidelines, if only one of the two policies covering the same loss has a COB provision, the plan (with / without) such a provision is the primary policy.

61. Marian Edwards is covered by her employer's group health insurance plan, which also covers her husband Dan and their children. In addition, Dan is covered by his employer's group plan, which covers Marian and their children. In the following questions, assume that all policies have COB provisions and that NAIC guidelines are followed.

    a. Marian incurs a loss covered by both policies. Which is the primary policy?

    b. Marian and Dan's son Phil incurs a loss covered by both policies. The primary policy is that of (the father / the mother / the older parent / the parent whose birthday falls earlier in the year).

    c. Marian was previously married to Jeff, and they have a daughter Patricia, of whom Marian has custody. Patricia is covered as a dependent by Marian's policy, Dan's policy, and Jeff s policy. If Patricia incurs a loss covered by all three policies, which policy is primary? Which is secondary? Which is third?

62. Which of these statements is true?

    • The implementation of coordination of benefits costs more in extra claim administration time than it saves in reduced claim payments, but it is necessary to eliminate incentives to use unneeded services.

    • The implementation of coordination of benefits costs about the same in extra claim administration time as it saves in reduced claim payments, but it is necessary to eliminate incentives to use unneeded services.

    • The implementation of coordination of benefits costs much less in extra claim administration time than it saves in reduced claim payments, so it both cuts claim costs directly and eliminates incentives to use unneeded services.

Paying a Benefit or Denying a Claim (Pages 50–51)

63. The insured is informed in writing of the decision on a claim (only if the claim is denied / only if a benefit is paid / whether the claim is denied or a benefit paid).

♦ 64. The standard form notifying an insured of a claim decision is the _____.

65. To pay a benefit, two pieces of information are needed: the amount of payment and _____.

66. Whether a benefit is paid to the insured or the provider is determined by the _____ and any _____ the insured may have made.

67. If an assignment of benefits is made, benefits (always / usually / never) go to a provider.

68. During a calendar year, MWR Insurance Company pays a total of $500 in benefits to a physician, Dr. Paul Chapel, Must MWR report this to the IRS?

Claim Investigations (Page 51)

69. When an examiner sees indications that a claim is inaccurate or questionable in some substantial way, _____ of the claim is initiated.

Hospital Audits (Page 51)

70. Many insurance companies audit hospital bills to verify that _____ and that _____.

71. In a hospital audit, all bills over a certain amount are (audited / reviewed to determine whether an audit is indicated / either, depending on the company).

72. Auditing may be done by (insurer employees / personnel of independent auditing companies / insureds / all of these).

Claim Administration and Customer Service (Page 52)

73. Why is claim administration so important to customer satisfaction?

74. How can each of these affect customer satisfaction?

    a. Telephone lines to the claim department.

    b. Personnel of claim customer service units.

    c. Explanations of benefits.

75. The goal of customer service should be the satisfaction not only of individual insureds but also of _____, _____, and _____.

Summary (Page 52)

76. The processing of a health insurance claim can be divided into three main steps. Describe each:

    a. The claim examiner confirms the status of coverage.

    b. The examiner determines if the specific loss claimed is covered by the policy.

    c. The examiner calculates the amount of benefit payment.

Answers

1. Whether a benefit is due to the insured; what the amount of that benefit is.

2. Facts of the case and the provisions of the policy.

3. The circumstances surrounding illness and injury and their treatment may be complicated; there is a great diversity of health insurance policies and each has a large number of provisions.

4. • Was the policy in effect when the insured incurred a loss?

   • Is the particular loss the insured incurred covered by the policy?

   • What amount of benefit does the policy pay for this loss?

5. Status of coverage

6. • When exactly did the loss occur?

   • Had coverage begun at that time?

   • Had coverage lapsed or ended at that time?

7. Group; individual.

8. The group policy; the coverage of the individual group member.

9. Checking status of coverage.

10. A medical condition began.

11. Medical treatment was first sought.

12. July. If a person delays seeking medical attention when it is clearly needed, the onset of the condition is considered to have occurred when symptoms were such that an ordinarily prudent person would have sought treatment.

13. Effective date of coverage.

14. Group.

15. Individual.

16. Normally the applicant must have paid the first premium; in some cases, he must have submitted a medical examination report that the insurer finds acceptable.

17. Both individual and group policies.

18. Whether the policy is reinstated or not.

19. Both individual and group policies.

20. Group policies only.

21. After the date of reinstatement.

22. More than 10 days after the date of reinstatement.

23. Made material misrepresentations in the application for insurance.

24. A false statement.

25. Would have refused to offer coverage or would have offered it on substantially different terms.

26. An existing or past medical condition.

27. Rescinds.

28. Add that provision to the policy, effective retroactively to the date of issue.

29. Contestable period; two or three years (usually two, but three in some states).

30. • What health care services or supplies is the insured making a claim for?

    • Are these services and supplies covered by the benefit provisions of the insured's policy?

    • Are there any other provisions of the policy that would make benefits not payable?

31. Reviewing the claim form, bills, and any other documents that have been submitted; putting them in order; and confirming that all bills pertain to the person making the claim and the condition reported on the claim form.

32. Benefit.

33. Exclusions, elimination periods, benefit periods, and overall maximums.

34. Are not usual for the medical condition of the claim and so may not be medically necessary.

35. Treatments and services usually provided, average length of hospital stay, and average duration of disability, if any.

36. Recognized health care professional groups and publications, agencies of the federal government, and insurer claim data.

37. Lump-sum payments and per-day hospital benefits.

38. Maximum dollar amounts for given expenses.

39. The amount charged by the provider, as long as the amount charged does not exceed eligible charge limits.

40. Normally charged for that service or a similar service by similar health care providers in the same geographic area.

41. May be defined in either way, depending on the policy.

42. The amount of the eligible charge limit.

43. By each insurance company for that company.

44. Bodies of data; methods of analysis.

45. Insurers.

46. Reports sent to insurers who subscribe to the service.

47. Service and geographic area.

48. Combine PHCS data with their own claim data.

49. Deductibles, coinsurance, or copayments; coordination of benefits (COB).

50. Overinsurance.

51. • A person may have two individual health insurance policies with overlapping coverage.

    • A person covered by her employer's group health plan may also have an individual policy.

    • A person covered by an employer's group plan may also be covered by a second group plan through a second employer or a professional association.

    • A husband and wife may both have employer-sponsored group health coverage that includes dependent coverage, so that both of them, as well as any dependent children, are covered by both plans.

52. • It leads to claim payments that are higher than needed to meet the legitimate needs of insureds.

    • It gives insureds financial incentives to use health care services that they do not need.

53. Overlap.

54. The amount of expenses incurred.

55. Primarily for group policies but also for some individual policies.

56. Losses covered by two (or more) policies; the responsibility for payment between one insurer and another.

57. What benefits Felicity's policy will pay.

58. The National Association of Insurance Commissioners (NAIC).

59. All the benefits it would normally pay if there were no additional coverage.

60. Without.

61. a. Marian's. (A person's own policy is primary and a policy covering her as a dependent is secondary.)

    b. The parent whose birthday falls earlier in the year.

    c. Marian's is primary, Dan's is secondary, and Jeff's is third.

62. The implementation of coordination of benefits costs much less in extra claim administration time than it saves in reduced claim payments, so it both cuts claim costs directly and eliminates incentives to use unneeded services.

63. Whether the claim is denied or a benefit paid.

64. Explanation of benefits (EOB).

65. The party to whom payment should be made.

66. Provisions of the policy; assignments of benefits.

67. Usually. (They may be paid to another party such as a creditor.)

68. No, annual benefits payments must exceed $600 for an insurer to be required to submit a report.

69. An investigation.

70. The services and supplies charged for were actually provided; the amounts charged are correct.

71. Either, depending on the company.

72. All of these.

73. Insureds often have more contact with an insurer's claim department than with any other part of the company.

74. a. Toll-free lines can increase accessibility.

    b. Qualified personnel ensure that insureds' questions are answered correctly.

   c. EOBs must be clearly written and promptly sent to avoid confusion and bad feeling on the part of insureds.

75. Group policyholder personnel, physicians and hospital staff, and insurance agents.

76. a. The examiner ascertains the date of the loss and the dates when coverage began and ended to determine whether coverage was in effect at the time of the loss. She must also note any indications that the policy may not be valid.

   b. She examines the benefit provisions and other provisions of the policy and also confirms that all services provided were necessary.

   c. She takes into account the provisions of the policy and sometimes the normal charges for services. She also considers any contributions owed by the insured and any benefit, payments made by other policies.

8 DISABILITY INCOME CLAIMS

Introduction (Page 53)

1. The handling of claims for disability income insurance differs in several ways from that of most kinds of health insurance because disability benefits do not compensate for _____ but rather for _____.

2. Disability benefit payments normally take the form of _____.

Processing a Disability Claim (Pages 53–55)

3. The focus of disability claim processing is establishing whether _____.

4. If a claimant is disabled, she is _____.

5. In a disability claim, the claimant normally submits proof of loss by _____.

6. For disability claims, provider bills are not usually submitted to establish proof of loss. This is because for disability income insurance, proof of loss means proof that _____, not proof that _____.

7. An insurer's disability claim form includes statements by _____ and _____. It also sometimes includes statements by _____ and _____.

8. The attending physician's statement on a disability claim form describes _____, evaluates _____, and in some cases estimates _____.

9. An employer's statement on a disability claim form indicates the _____ and _____ the claimant stopped working.

10. In the disability claim process, as for other coverages, the claim examiner first checks status of coverage to make sure the claimant was _____.

11. The disability claim examiner must also review the provisions of the policy to make sure coverage is not disallowed for some reason, such as _____.

12. Individual disability income policies (treat injuries and illness the same / cover injuries but not illnesses / cover both injuries and illnesses but provide different benefits for them / may treat illnesses and injuries in any of these ways, depending on the policy).

13. Give two reasons why disability is not a purely medical question.

14. Disability claims are generally subject to greater scrutiny than other kinds of claims because _____.

15. An insurer can pay a very large total amount for a single disability claim because the benefits for a disability claim take the form of _____.

16. The claim examiner must contact the attending physician for more information if _____ or if _____.

17. A claim examiner for Great Plains Insurance Company questions the attending physician report for a disability claimant, Tom Grosvenor. Great Plains notifies Tom that it wants him to be examined by a physician it has selected. Tom refuses. Which of these statements is true?

    • Great Plains may request an additional examination by Tom's own physician or more information from her, but it may not require Tom to be examined by a physician it selects.

    • Great Plains may require Tom to be examined by a physician agreed to by both parties, but it may not require him to be examined by a physician it selects.

    • Great Plains may require Tom to be examined by a physician it selects.

◆ 18. When a disability claimant is examined by a physician selected by the insurer, this is known as _____.

19. If a claimant refuses to be examined by a physician selected by the insurer, the insurer may _____.

20. Why is prompt examination of disability claims so important?

Continuing Review of Disability Claims (Pages 55–56)

21. Disability benefit payments are usually made every month (or week) until _____ or until _____.

22. During the period when benefits are being paid, the examiner must periodically review the case to determine _____.

23. The claim examiner normally verifies that disability is continuing by periodically requesting and reviewing _____.

◆ 24. In some cases, an insured is no longer totally disabled and can work, but due to a continuing condition he is not able to earn as much as before disability. This situation is known as _____ or _____.

25. In the situation described above, benefits are paid to make up for part of the insured's loss in earnings by (all / some) disability income policies.

26. In a case of residual disability, why must the claim examiner obtain accurate information in each of the following areas?

   a. The insured's predisability earnings.

   b. The insured's current earnings.

   c. The insured's medical condition.

♦ 27. A maximum period of time during which benefits will be paid is known as a _____ period.

28. An insured may go through periods of disability separated by times when she is not disabled. A separate benefit period may apply to each period of disability, or one benefit period may apply to all the disability periods combined, depending on _____.

29. Douglas Weaver has a disability income policy with a benefit period of two years. Douglas suffered an injury, was disabled for 15 months, and then returned to work. He worked for three months, then went on disability again, and has now been on disability for four months. If the two periods are considered separate claims, how much longer can Douglas receive benefits under the policy?

30. In the case above, if both periods of disability are considered part of the same claim, how much longer can Douglas receive benefits under the policy?

31. Determining whether two periods of disability are part of one claim or two is (usually clear-cut / often complicated).

32. Determining whether two periods of disability are part of one claim or two depends on _____ and _____.

Tax Withholding from Benefits (Page 56)

33. Federal legislation requires insurers to withhold federal income tax from disability benefit payments (in all cases / at the request of the insured).

34. Federal legislation requires insurers to withhold Social Security taxes from disability benefit payments in (all / some) cases.

Summary (Page 57)

35. Explain how claim administration for disability income insurance differs from that of most other kinds of health insurance in these main areas:

   a. Focus of the claim process.

   b. Degree of scrutiny.

   c. Continuing review.

   d. Income considerations.

Answers

1. Medical expenses; lost income.

2. Monthly payments of a preset amount.

3. The claimant is disabled.

4. Unable to work due to an illness or injury.

5. Completing the insurer's claim form.

6. The claimant is disabled, not proof that he has incurred any specific medical expense.

7. The claimant and the attending physician; other health care providers and the employer.

8. The illness or injury; the claimant's condition and ability to work; the length of time the insured will not be able to work.

9. Date and reason.

10. Covered by the policy at the time of loss.

11. Exclusions of disabilities due to certain causes (such as a preexisting condition or a self-inflicted injury) or different treatment for injuries and illnesses.

12. May treat illnesses and injuries in any of these ways, depending on the policy.

13. • Whether a person is unable to work depends not only on her medical condition but also on the duties of her occupation.

    • Whether a person is disabled under the terms of a policy depends on the definition of disability contained in that policy, and this definition varies.

14. The amounts involved can be very large.

15. Monthly payments that are often of substantial amounts and may continue for a long period of time.

16. The attending physician's statement is inadequate or unclear in any way or if the claim diverges from norms in any way.

17. Great Plains may require Tom to be examined by a physician it selects.

18. An independent medical examination.

19. Delay the processing of the claim and the payment of benefits until he does so.

20. If a claim is not examined until the insured has recovered and returned to work, it may be difficult to determine if the claim was valid.

21. The insured ceases to be disabled, or until the insured reaches the maximum amount of time or money allowed under the policy.

22. Whether the insured is still disabled.

23. Reports from the attending physician.

24. Residual disability or permanent partial disability.

25. Some.

26. a. Benefits are based on the amount of lost ncome, and that amount is calculated by subtracting the insured's current earnings from his predisability earnings.

    b. If the insured's current earnings increase, the insured's disability-related loss of income is reduced, and his benefits, which are intended to compensate for that loss, must also be reduced.

    c. It must be confirmed that the insured's reduced earnings are in fact due to his medical condition.

27. Benefit.

28. Whether the periods of disability are considered to be all part of one claim or each part of a separate claim.

29. 20 months. (He has only been on disability for the latest claim for four months, so he has 20 months left in his 24-month benefit period.)

30. Five months. (He has been on disability for one claim for a total of 19 months, and his benefit period is 24 months.)

31. Often complicated.

32. The precise language of the policy and the facts of the individual case.

33. At the request of the insured.

34. Some.

35. a. In processing disability claims, the focus is on determining whether the claimant is disabled, not on examining expenses

    b. Because of the very large amounts of benefits that are often at stake, disability claims are usually given closer scrutiny than other claims.

c. Since disability benefit payments continue as long as the insured is disabled, the case must be periodically reviewed to confirm that the disability persists.

d. To determine the amount of residual disability benefits, the examiner must take into account the insured's income.

9 CONTROLLING OPERATIONAL COSTS

Introduction (Page 59)

1. How are health insurance premiums affected by the rise in health care costs?

2. What are the two main consequences of increases in health insurance premiums?

3. Describe the impact of higher health insurance premiums on the following:

   a. Businesses.

   b. Individuals.

4. Which of these statements most accurately reflects the trends of recent years?

   - The number of people with health insurance has grown, and the number of people without health insurance has declined.

   - The number of people with health insurance has declined, and the number of people without health insurance has grown.

   - The number of people with health insurance and the number of people without health insurance have both grown.

5. Health insurance companies have taken two main approaches in working to control costs and keep premiums down. What are they?

Controlling Marketing, Sales, and Issuance Costs (Page 60)

6. This year, Monmouth Insurance Company has a large number of continuing policies and a relatively small number of new policies. Nimrod Insurance Company, on the other hand, has a much larger proportion of new policies. Which company is likely to have greater expenses in the area of marketing, selling, and issuance?

7. If a company has high marketing, selling, and issuance expenses, it should (make less effort to sell new policies / make a greater effort to get existing policyholders to continue their policies / both).

8. The degree to which policyholders continue their policies is known as _____.

9. In the initial sale of a policy, sales personnel can improve the likelihood that the policy will be continued by _____.

10. After the initial sale, sales personnel can improve persistency by maintaining close contact with policyholders. This enables them to do three things. What are they?

11. Insurers can get their sales personnel to act in ways that encourage persistency primarily by means of _____.

Controlling Underwriting Costs (Page 60)

12. What are some of the causes of the increase in underwriting costs?

13. Underwriting costs are particularly high for individual insurance because _____.

14. How can underwriting costs be reduced in each of these ways?

    a. Application processing.

    b. Use of technology.

    c. Training.

Controlling Claim Processing Costs (Pages 61–62)

15. How can insurers reduce the cost of processing claims in each of these ways?

    a. Use of senior claim personnel.

    b. Organization of claim offices.

    c. Technology.

16. Which of the three approaches listed above has had the greatest impact?

17. Claim administration is an activity that is well suited to computerization because it involves _____ and _____.

♦ 18. Describe what each of these technologies does:

    a. Imaging.

    b. Scanning.

    c. Electronic claim processing.

    d. Fraud detection software.

    e. Expert disability system.

    f. Automated repetitive payment system.

19. Imaging cuts claim costs by allowing a shift from a _____ filing system to a less labor-intensive _____ filing system.

20. Scanning cuts claim costs by eliminating many hours spent on _____.

21. In electronic claim processing, electronic fraud detection, and expert disability systems, a computer makes decisions by _____.

22. An automated repetitive payment system is used most often to make (medical expense / dental / disability income) payments.

Other Cost-Cutting Technology (Page 62)

23. The scanning systems used for claim forms can also be used for _____ forms

24. A technology that cuts customer service personnel costs is _____.

25. Two technologies that make communication quicker, more effective, and cheaper are _____ and _____.

Answers

1. Rises in health care costs lead to increases in the claims made to health insurance companies and consequently in the premiums that insurers must charge in order to pay those claims.

2. • Individuals and businesses must spend a larger portion of their earnings on health insurance.

    • The number of people without health insurance is greater than it would otherwise be.

3. a. Many businesses can no longer afford to provide group insurance to their employees.

    b. Many individuals can no longer afford to pay the premiums of either group or individual policies.

4. The number of people with health insurance and the number of people without health insurance have both grown.

5. Insurers have sought to make their own operations as efficient as possible, and they have structured their coverages to promote the cost-effective use of health care services.

6. Nimrod.

7. Make a greater effort to get existing policyholders to continue their policies.

8. Persistency.

9. Making sure that the policy meets the policyholder's specific needs.

10. • Reinforcing the policyholder's recognition of the need to continue the coverage;

    • being aware of any problems that arise and addressing them; and

    • being aware of any changes in the needs of the policyholder and suggesting modifications and additions in coverage to meet those needs.

11. Training.

12. Higher salaries, rising overhead costs, and increases in the cost of medical examinations of applicants, attending physician statements, and inspection reports.

13. Each insured must be underwritten separately.

14. a. Implementing an efficient and time-saving application processing system.

    b. Introducing computerized systems that analyze underwriting data to determine if human intervention is needed.

    c. Focusing on training employees in the proper initial handling of applications, which can eliminate or substantially reduce delays and additional costs.

15. a. Claim processing units should be organized so that highly paid senior claim personnel deal only with the small number of claims with complex problems.

    b. Claim operations can be concentrated in one large central office.

    c. Computerized systems can perform electronic transmission of claims, automatic calculation of benefits, and automatic payment of claims.

16. Technology.

17. Rule-based decision-making and the processing of a high volume of transactions.

18. a. Converts paper documents into electronic documents that can be stored, retrieved, and viewed by computer.

b. Converts paper documents into electronic documents that can be stored, retrieved, and viewed by computer; it also converts data from paper forms and documents into electronic data that a computerized claim system can process.

c. Enables a computer, with little or no human involvement, to determine whether benefits should be paid and what the amount should be; to produce benefit checks, explanations of benefits, and necessary letters; and to store information about the claim.

d. Enables a computer to identify claims with characteristics that are often associated with fraud.

e. Enables a computer to estimate the duration of a disability.

f. Automatically pays benefits on a regular basis for a predetermined period of time.

19. Paper; automated computerized.

20. Data entry (converting paper data to electronic data).

21. Applying a set of rules to the data of a claim.

22. Disability income.

23. Enrollment.

24. Automated voice response systems (AVRS).

25. Electronic mail (e-mail) and insurer Internet sites.

10 PROMOTING COST-EFFECTIVE HEALTH CARE

Introduction (Pages 63–64)

1. The main cause of the increase in the cost of health insurance is (rising administrative costs / rising health care costs).

2. Health care costs can be cut (only by not providing people with the best medical care available / by providing the best health care available in the most efficient and least wasteful way possible).

3. In practice, providing high-quality, cost-effective health care means doing two things. What are they?

4. Insurers can promote cost-effective health care by encouraging (consumers / health care providers / both) to make cost-effective choices.

Cost Sharing (Page 64)

5. In cost sharing, insureds have a financial incentive to avoid using unnecessary services because they (pay a penalty for using such services / receive cash awards for not using such services / pay a portion of the cost of all services).

6. Cost sharing arrangements include _____, _____, and _____.

7. Zoe Smith incurs hospital expenses of $800. Her medical expense policy requires her to pay the first $500 of covered expenses before the insurer pays benefits. This is an example of what form of cost sharing?

8. After Zoe pays the first $500 of covered expenses, she pays 20 percent of remaining covered expenses, and her insurer pays the other 80 percent. This is an example of what form of cost sharing?

9. When Zoe sees her physician, she always pays $20 for the visit, regardless of the actual cost of the visit. This is an example of what form of cost sharing?

10. A (coinsurance payment / copayment) is a flat dollar amount regardless of actual costs.

11. A (coinsurance payment / copayment) is a percentage of costs.

12. In coinsurance, the insured typically pays (5 or 10 / 20 or 25 / 40 or 50 / 75 or 80) percent of expenses.

13. Cost sharing (is a recently developed approach / has been practiced for many years).

14. In recent years, insurers have (increased / decreased) cost sharing.

Targeted Incentives for Cost-Effective Alternatives
(Pages 65–66)

15. Cost sharing is a (broad / targeted) approach to encouraging cost-effective choices.

16. Cost sharing normally gives insureds incentives to (hold down their health care expenditures in a general way / use or not use particular services or treatments / both).

17. When insurers use targeted incentives for cost-effective alternatives, they identify _____ and give insureds incentives to choose _____.

18. The use of outpatient care and outpatient surgery reduces costs by eliminating the high costs of _____.

19. Outpatient surgery is becoming safe and appropriate in an increasing number of cases, as new surgical techniques and anesthetics allow _____.

20. Insurers often give insureds incentives to use outpatient surgery by _____ if surgery is performed on an outpatient basis.

21. Birthing centers are an alternative to hospitalization for _____ and _____.

22. What do many insurers do to encourage the use of birthing centers?

23. Treatment in a specialized drug and alcohol treatment facility is more likely to result in long-term recovery than hospital treatment because, while both provide _____, specialized facilities also offer _____.

24. Hospice care is an alternative to hospital care for (terminally ill patients only / all seriously ill patients).

25. Of the following goals, which ones are a focus of hospice care? Curing the patient / relieving the patient's pain and discomfort / prolonging the patient's life / addressing the patient's emotional and spiritual needs.

26. **Centers of excellence** are an alternative to general hospital care for patients with (terminal illnesses / serious illnesses / difficult-to-treat or rare illnesses / patients whose primary need is nursing care).

27. Centers of excellence are distinctive for providing (rehabilitation services / nursing care services / advanced treatments).

28. Centers of excellence offer (high-quality care / economical care / both).

29. Why are certain treatments often less expensive in centers of excellence than in general hospitals?

30. Skilled nursing facilities and home health care are appropriate for persons who do not need _____ but do need _____.

31. In the past, people often remained in a hospital unnecessarily because their insurance _____.

32. Home health care is usually appropriate for patients who need (more / less) care than that provided by a skilled nursing facility.

33. Home health care is provided by _____ or _____, working under the supervision of a _____.

34. Generally, (hospital care / home health care / skilled nursing facility care) is the most expensive, and (hospital care / home health care / skilled nursing facility care) is the least expensive.

35. Home health care is an option for an (increasing / decreasing) number of people.

Case Management (Pages 66–68)

36. Case management is a method of improving the (quality of health care / cost-effectiveness of health care / both).

37. Case management promotes cost-effectiveness primarily by (encouraging insureds to make cost-effective choices / identifying and eliminating redundant and overlapping health care services / both).

38. Case management addresses (overlapping of health care services / gaps in health care services / both).

39. Case management addresses a lack of coordination of services caused by _____.

40. Case management is typically used for people with _____ or _____ medical conditions.

41. In case management, a (physician / nurse / hospital administrator) is usually given the responsibility of monitoring and coordinating services provided to the patient.

42. Which of the following is true?

    • Case management is appropriate only in a few cases, but it can save a lot of money in those cases.

    • Case management is appropriate only in a few cases, and it can save only a moderate amount of money in those cases.

    • Case management is appropriate in many cases, and it can save a lot of money in those cases.

    • Case management is appropriate in many cases, but it can save only a moderate amount of money in those cases.

43. Overall, the potential of savings of case management is (small / moderate / great).

44. Insurance companies flag cases as possibly appropriate to case management in what three circumstances?

45. Case management may be initiated by (the insurer / a provider / an insured or her family / any of these).

46. In case management, improvements in quality of care and cost savings are maximized if the case is identified (at the first hospital admission / after three hospital admissions / before the first hospital admission).

47. Most insurers (require / do not require) insureds to participate in case management.

48. What advantages does case management offer insureds in each of these areas

    a. Relations with providers.

    b. Decision making.

    c. Coverage.

Wellness Programs (Page 68)

49. The methods of controlling health care costs previously discussed in this chapter work by _____. Wellness programs differ in that they work by _____.

50. How can people make certain medical conditions less likely?

51. How can people keep certain medical conditions from becoming a serious problem?

52. What are the two main services typically offered by wellness programs?

53. Some wellness programs sponsored jointly by insurers and employers offer some financial assistance to insureds who participate in programs for _____, _____, or _____.

54. Wellness programs can (improve health only / both improve health and cut health care costs).

Summary (Pages 68–69)

55. The most effective way for insurers to hold premium rates down is to (control their operational costs / promote the practice of high quality, cost-effective health care).

Answers

1. Rising health care costs.

2. By providing the best health care available in the most efficient and least wasteful way possible.

3. • Using the most effective means of diagnosis and treatment while at the same time avoiding unnecessary medical services; and

    • in cases in which two alternative treatments are possible, both equally effective from a medical point of view but not equally economical, taking the more economical approach.

4. Both.

5. Pay a portion of the cost of all services.

6. Deductibles, coinsurance, and copayments.

7. A deductible.

8. Coinsurance.

9. A copayment.

10. Copayment.

11. Coinsurance payment.

12. 20 or 25 percent.

13. Has been practiced for many years.

14. Increased.

15. Broad.

16. Hold down their health care expenditures in a general way.

17. Specific health care services that are cost-effective and others that are not; the cost-effective alternatives.

18. Hospital room and board.

19. Quick recovery.

20. Reducing deductibles and coinsurance.

21. Low-risk deliveries and postpartum newborn care.

22. They waive deductibles and/or coinsurance.

23. Detoxification; counseling.

24. Terminally ill patients only.

25. Relieving the patient's pain and discomfort and addressing the patient's emotional and spiritual needs.

26. Difficult-to-treat or rare illnesses.

27. Advanced treatments.

28. Both.

29. Because centers of excellence specialize in and perform those treatments more frequently than general hospitals.

30. Hospital care; some professional care.

31. Only paid for hospitalization.

32. Less.

33. Visiting nurses or home health aides; registered nurse.

34. Hospital care is most expensive; home health care is least expensive.

35. Increasing.

36. Both.

37. Identifying and eliminating redundant and overlapping health care services.

38. Both.

39. Many different providers.

40. Catastrophic or long-term.

41. Nurse.

42. Case management is appropriate only in a few cases, but it can save a lot of money in those cases.

43. Great.

44. • A single claim is above a certain amount.

    • The claims for any individual total more than a certain amount.

    • A claim is made for one of a list of specified medical conditions.

45. Any of these.

46. Before the first hospital admission.

47. Do not require.

48. a. Case management helps the insured deal with many different providers.

b. Case management gives the insured a full understanding of her choices at each stage and assists her in making decisions.

c. Some case management programs provide coverage for services that the regular health insurance plan does not.

49. Ensuring that health care services are provided in a cost-effective way; helping people avoid becoming ill.

50. By avoiding behaviors such as smoking, drinking to excess, overeating, eating an unhealthy diet, and failing to exercise.

51. By getting regular examinations and testing so that the conditions can be detected and treated early.

52. • Information on how behavior and lifestyle affect health and how to make changes.

   • Physical examinations and disease screening.

53. Losing weight, quitting smoking, or improving fitness.

54. Both improve health and cut health care costs.

55. Promote the practice of high-quality, cost-effective health care.

11 HEALTH INSRANCE FRAUD AND ABUSE

Defining Fraud and Abuse (Pages 71–72)

✦ 1. What is the definition of **health insurance fraud**?

✦ 2. What is the definition of **health insurance abuse**?

3. Todd Emery fills out and submits to his insurer a claim form stating that he received a certain medical service, but he did not in fact receive this service. Todd is committing (health insurance fraud / health insurance abuse / neither).

4. Dr. Arbuthnot, a physician, routinely has all new patients undergo a number of tests, even though several of these test are appropriate only for persons with certain conditions. Dr. Arbuthnot is committing (health insurance fraud / health insurance abuse / neither).

5. In a case of (fraud only / abuse only / either fraud or abuse / neither fraud nor abuse), a crime has occurred and a criminal prosecution may be pursued.

6. In a case of (fraud only / abuse only / either fraud or abuse / neither fraud nor abuse), the insurer may seek to recover benefits that should not have been paid.

Provider Fraud and Abuse (Pages 72–75)

✦ 7. When a provider charges an insurer for a service she did not in fact provide or charges too much for a service that was provided, this is known as a _____.

8. Each billing code corresponds to a _____.

9. Billing codes were devised to make (fraud more difficult / claim processing more efficient / medical costs more uniform).

10. *The Physicians' Current Procedural Terminology* provides detailed descriptions of _____.

11. *The Physicians' Current Procedural Terminology* is published by (the U.S. Department of Health and Human Services / the American Medical Association / the Health Insurance Association of America).

12. Why is fraud involving billing codes often not detected?

✦ 13. In the following cases, which of these billing schemes is being used? **Billing for services not provided / billing for noncovered treatments / upcoding / unbundling of charges.**

a. Nora Bailey has a routine visit with her physician, who bills her insurer for an extensive office visit.

b. Dr. Caligari, a surgeon, performed minor surgery in his office. He bills the patient's insurer for the correct surgical procedure, but he charges for the use of operating room equipment that he did not use.

c. Dr. English performs a neurological operation that includes a number of surgical procedures. She bills the insurer for each of these procedures as if she had performed them at separate times.

d. Dr. Forsyth performs a limited physical examination of Bob Conway and charges for a comprehensive physical exam.

e. Merlin Medical Laboratory performs 13 tests on Joanne Wilson. It submits a bill to her insurer for those 13 tests and also for two other tests that were not performed.

f. A staff member of Whole Life Clinic performs acupuncture on Tom Collier. Since acupuncture is not covered by Tom's insurance, Whole Life bills using a code for physical therapy.

14. Why is submitting a bill for a service that is similar to but more expensive than the service actually provided called upcoding?

♦ 15. Procedures and medicines that have not been tested and established by the proper professional or regulatory authorities as effective and safe are known as _____, _____, or _____ treatments.

♦ 16. In **overutilization** of services, providers bill for services they (provide unnecessarily / do not provide).

17. Overutilization is most commonly a form of (fraud / abuse). Why?

18. In the following cases, state whether the provider (is / is not / may or may not be) committing health insurance abuse.

a. Ellen Gorman is kept in the hospital several days longer than is normal for someone with her medical condition.

b. Dr. Offenbach repeatedly provides services that, according to guidelines established by medical experts, are not necessary, and when he is questioned he is able to offer no justification.

c. Dr. Pollini requires a patient to continue therapy longer than medical experts believe is necessary because it is her honest medical judgment that continued therapy *is* necessary.

d. Dr. Lewis has a policy of requiring all new patients to undergo a large number of tests, even though some of these tests are not appropriate for most people.

19. Dr. Kelly has Tim Bates undergo a test that she knows to be unnecessary. She does this because she fears that if she does not and Tim's condition does not improve, he may bring a malpractice suit against her. This is an example of _____.

20. Dr. Phelan advertises that he does not require patients to pay deductibles, copayments, or coinsurance payments. This practice (constitutes / does not constitute / may or may not constitute) fraud or abuse.

21. In cases where the waiving of out-of-pocket payments is legal, why is it often associated with fraud and abuse?

Consumer Fraud and Abuse (Pages 75–76)

22. Health insurance benefits are now most often paid to (providers / insureds).

23. How can an insured gain by submitting a false bill?

24. How can an insured gain by submitting an altered bill?

25. Claims filed against U.S. insurers by persons in (the U.S. / foreign countries) are more likely to include false or altered bills.

 26. A person deliberately buys many policies covering the same expenses and then submits claims for the same loss under all these policies with the intention of making a substantial amount of money. This sort of scheme is known as _____.

27. Coordination of benefits does not prevent the scheme described in the preceding question because the insured does not _____ as she is required to do.

28. Disability income insurance fraud usually involves misrepresentations related to three things. What are they?

29. Whether someone is able to work or not is (usually clear-cut / often ambiguous).

30. If an insurance policy has a vague definition of disability, it is (easier / harder) to prove that an insured is not disabled.

31. A policy can define disability less vaguely by specifying _____ and _____.

32. The benefit amounts are greater, so the temptation of fraud is greater for (medical expense / disability insurance).

Motor Vehicle Accidents (Pages 76–77)

33. How do fraudulent schemes involving actual motor vehicle accidents work?

 34. What happens in a **paper accident**?

35. In the above two schemes, how are participants able to document their phony injuries?

✦ 36. A secret collaboration of two or more parties for fraudulent purposes is a _____.

Answers

1. A person knowingly and intentionally deceives another in order to gain a health insurance benefit that he is not legitimately entitled to.

2. A person seeks to obtain benefits that she is not entitled to, but she does not knowingly and intentionally deceive or make any misrepresentations.

3. Fraud. Todd is knowingly and intentionally making a misrepresentation.

4. Abuse. It is not fraud, because Dr. Arbothnot is not making any misrepresentation—he is simply billing for tests he did in fact perform. It is abuse, because Dr. Arbothnot is intentionally trying to increase his earnings in an illegitimate way.

5. Fraud only.

6. Either fraud or abuse.

7. Billing scheme.

8. Medical or surgical service or procedure.

9. Claim processing more efficient.

10. The services and procedures that correspond to each billing code.

11. The American Medical Association.

12. Because coded bills are usually processed by standardized procedures or automated systems.

13. a. Upcoding.

 b. Billing for services not provided.

 c. Unbundling of charges.

 d. Upcoding.

 e. Billing for services not provided. f. Billing for noncovered treatments.

14. Because the bill uses the code for a higher-priced service instead of the correct code.

15. Unproven, alternative, or experimental treatments.

16. Provide unnecessarily.

17. Abuse. The provider does not usually misrepresent the services she has provided or the patient's condition.

18. a. May or may not be. (There may be complications or unusual circumstances that justify the longer hospitalization.)

 b. Is.

 c. Is not. Dr. Pollini is overutilizing, because she is providing unneeded services, but she is not committing abuse because she is not overutilizing with the purpose of financial gain.

 d. s.

19. Defensive medicine.

20. May or may not. Sometimes this practice violates regulations or contracts, but not always.

21. Many of the providers who waive out-of-pocket payments use fraudulent activities to offset the cost.

22. Providers.

23. If benefits are paid to the insured, she can submit a false bill for services she never received and never paid for and pocket the money paid by the insurer.

24. He alters the provider's bills to show that he received more expensive services than those actually provided. He is reimbursed for the higher-priced service, reimburses the provider for the cheaper service, and keeps the difference.

25. Foreign countries.

26. Insurance speculation.

27. Report each policy to the insurers providing the other policies.

28. • The insured's ability to work;

 • the insured's income; and * the cause of the disability.

29. Often ambiguous.

30. Harder.

31. What work duties an insured can and cannot perform and what alternative occupations are acceptable.

32. Disability insurance.

33. People deliberately cause accidents and falsely claim injuries.

34. People report an accident that did not occur and falsely claim injuries.

35. A provider is involved in the scheme.

36. Collusion.

12 PREVENTING FRAUD AND ABUSE

Insurer Anti-Fraud Measures (Pages 79–80)

✦ 1. Claim personnel commonly examine claims as they are received for indications of possible errors or fraud. This is known as _____.

2. Claim personnel (sometimes detect fraud themselves / only identify cases in which fraud may be occurring and pass them to an investigator).

✦ 3. A group in an insurance company that has the primary responsibility of investigating suspicious claims is called a _____.

4. Which of these statements is true?

   - SIUs are becoming more common, but most insurers still do not have them.

   - SIUs are becoming more common, and most insurers now have them.

   - SIUs are becoming less common, but most insurers still have them.

   - SIUs are becoming less common, and few insurers still have them.

5. Some of the outside services that insurers use in the area of fraud include specialists in _____ and _____.

6. Why do insurers sometimes use outside services?

7. Databases useful in anti-fraud efforts are maintained by _____, _____, and _____.

8. Some insurers encourage insureds to report cases of fraud that come to their attention by maintaining _____.

9. Some insurers encourage insureds to audit their own bills by paying them _____.

10. In recent years, insurer anti-fraud efforts have (intensified / slackened / stayed about the same).

11. In recent years, anti-fraud efforts by government agencies have (intensified / slackened / stayed about the same).

12. List the main anti-fraud activities that insurers engage in.

Fraud Detection and Investigation (Pages 80–83)

✦ 13. There are certain characteristics of claims, such that a claim with one of these characteristics is more likely to be fraudulent than a claim without one. Such characteristics are known as _____.

14. Red flags are used by (claim personnel / computer programs / both).

15. If a claim has a red flag, the claim is (definitely fraudulent / more likely to be fraudulent than the average claim).

16. An investigation (by definition always involves / may or may not involve) the participation of outside investigators or law enforcement agencies.

17. An investigative report serves two purposes: It determines _____ _____, and it is the basis for _____.

18. In deciding whether the identification of fraudulent claims by claim personnel is worthwhile, insurers must balance _____ against _____.

19. In recent years, the work of identifying fraudulent claims has been made cheaper and less time-consuming by _____.

20. What are some red flags that are typical of false and altered bills?

21. Under what circumstances is specialized equipment necessary to detect false and altered bills?

22. The examination of physical documents is becoming (more / less) important.

23. Red flags used to screen electronic claims are related to _____ rather than the physical characteristics of documents.

24. Describe four red flags used in screening electronic claims.

25. Investigators review the medical records of the insureds to make sure the _____ and the _____ match the facts stated in the bill.

26. Cases of insurance speculation usually come to light when a claim examiner notices on the bill of a provider an indication of _____.

27. If insurance speculation is suspected, the investigator normally contacts _____ to verify that _____.

28. In cases of insurance speculation, the investigator is usually (hindered by the reluctance / helped by the willingness) of other insurers to share records and information.

29. Name four common characteristics of fraudulent claims involving motor vehicle accidents.

30. Why are soft tissue injuries often claimed in phony motor vehicle accidents?

31. Name some common characteristics of fraudulent foreign claims.

32. Firms specializing in foreign claim investigation are (normally based overseas / often based in the United States).

33. Insurers are particularly concerned with identifying disability income fraud because disability claims _____.

34. Describe four common steps that can be taken if a disability income claim is suspicious.

35. Why might an insurer be reluctant to take the four steps mentioned above?

36. In the investigation of disability income claims, surveillance of the insured is used to determine whether _____ indicates that the insured is able to work.

37. What public records are useful in claim investigations?

38. What kinds of information do investigators find in databases?

39. New technology has made databases even more useful in recent years by increasing _____ and making them easier to _____ and _____.

Government Involvement in Fraud Prevention (Pages 84–85)

40. Legal penalties for health insurance fraud include _____, _____, and _____.

41. Which statement is true about federal government efforts to combat health insurance fraud?

    • The FBI conducts all anti-fraud activities of the federal government.

    • Federal anti-fraud activities are conducted primarily by such agencies as the Department of Health and Human Services, and the FBI has very little involvement.

    • The FBI conducts some federal anti-fraud activities, but other federal agencies handle some types of fraud, and the FBI has no involvement or authority in these areas.

    • The FBI conducts some federal anti-fraud activities, and other federal agencies handle some types of fraud, but the FBI works with these other agencies and has the authority to investigate all types of fraud.

42. State fraud bureaus collect information from _____ on _____.

43. State fraud bureaus (are / are not) involved in the investigation of cases.

44. For what professions do state fraud bureaus promote anti-fraud training?

45. Insurers can provide state fraud bureaus with information without fear of being sued for libel or slander because _____.

46. State fraud bureaus often impose requirements on insurers involving _____, _____, and _____.

47. State fraud bureau requirements have created a burden for insurers because they are _____.

48. The federal government and state governments are influenced by model laws relating to insurance fraud drafted by _____.

49. HIPAA establishes a program to coordinate the efforts of _____ working to control health insurance fraud.

50. HIPAA requires (government agencies only / insurers only / both government agencies and insurers) to report _____.

51. HIPAA adds to the U.S. Code the _____. This pertains to fraud in (public / private / both public and private) health care benefit programs.

Insurance Industry Associations (Pages 85–86)

52. In general, insurers (share information, but do not investigate or prosecute cases together / share information and sometimes investigate cases together, but do not prosecute cases together / share information and sometimes investigate and prosecute cases together).

53. Which organization is described?

a.The national association representing companies providing health insurancecoverage, it is engaged in a number of efforts in the area of health insurance fraud and abuse.

b.An issue-based organization made up of private and public sector individuals and organizations and focusing on the detection, investigation, and prosecution of health care fraud.

c. An organization established to educate, inform, and encourage insurers to step up anti-fraud efforts.

54. Regional associations and task forces are typically made up of _____, _____, and _____. and they facilitate _____ and _____.

Answers

1. Screening.

2. Sometimes detect fraud themselves.

3. Special investigative unit (SIU).

4. SIUs are becoming more common, and most insurers now have them.

5. Surveillance and foreign claims.

6. It is not always economically feasible for insurers to develop specialized personnel or units that can handle all types of fraud investigation work.

7. Government agencies, independent bureaus, and commercial services.

8. Hotlines.

9. A share of any savings that may result.

10. Intensified.

11. Intensified.

12. Training employees; screening and auditing claims; creating special investigative units (SIUs); using outside services and databases ;and working with insureds, other insurers,

government entities, and law enforcement agencies.

13. Red flags.

14. Both.

15. More likely to be fraudulent than the average claim.

16. May or may not involve.

17. The insurer's action on the case; the insurer's legal case in a lawsuit or criminal prosecution.

18. The gains realized against the work hours spent.

19. Software screening programs.

20. Typewriter strike-overs, liquid paper corrections, different colored inks, non-matching fonts, missing signatures, photocopies instead of originals.

21. When they have been prepared by skilled criminals and so cannot be detected by the naked eye.

22. Less.

23. The facts of the case.

24. • Bills are shown as already paid in cash.

    • In a case where benefits would normally be assigned to a provider, they are unassigned and so must be paid directly to the insured.

    • The services claimed are inconsistent with the diagnosis.

    • Physicians' bills show many visits, but no prescription bills or other related expenses are submitted.

25. Condition of the patient and the health care services she received.

26. A second insurer that the insured did not declare.

27. The other insurance company; overinsurance in fact exists.

28. Helped by the willingness.

29. • Subjective injuries such as neck or back sprain are claimed.

    • Soft tissue injuries are claimed.

    • The same medical provider is used for many auto accident claims.

    • Police reports are filed at stations rather than at the scene of the accident.

30. Because they do not show up on X-rays.

31. Diagnosis of hepatitis; diagnosis of injuries resulting from a motor vehicle accident; lengthy hospital stays in Africa or the Middle East.

32. Often based in the United States.

33. Can involve very large amounts of money.

34. • The insurer requires the insured to submit to an independent medical examination.

    • The insurer requests and reviews medical records and reports from physicians on an on-going basis.

    • A case manager is hired to assess the authenticity of the disability and the abilities and needs of the insured.

    • Surveillance of the insured is conducted.

35. They are expensive.

36. The insured's behavior.

37. Court records, marriage and death records, and motor vehicle records.

38. Insurance policy numbers, claim histories, past convictions, or past suspicion of fraudulent activity.

39. The amount of information in them; use and access.

40. Monetary fines, prison sentences, and the revocation of professional licenses.

41. The FBI conducts some federal anti-fraud activities, and other federal agencies handle some types of health care fraud, but the FBI works with these other agencies and has the authority to investigate all types of fraud.

42. Insurance companies; suspicious claims.

43. Are.

44. Law enforcement personnel, insurer personnel, members of the media, judges, and prosecutors.

45. They are granted immunity from such suits for any information they submit.

46. The reporting of information, the staffing levels of SIUs, and the training of SIU staff and other insurer personnel.

47. Different for each state.

48. The National Association of Insurance Commissioners (NAIC).

49. Federal, state, and local law enforcement programs.

50. Both government agencies and insurers; any adverse action taken against a health care provider, supplier, or practitioner.

51. Federal offense of health care fraud; both public and private.

52. Share information and sometimes investigate and prosecute cases together.

53. a. America's Health Insurance Plans (AHIP).

b. The National Health Care Anti-Fraud Association (NHCAA).

c. The Fraud and Claim Abuse Committee of the International Claim Association (ICA).

54. Insurers, government entities, and law enforcement agencies; the sharing of information and the collaboration on cases.

13 PRICING HEALTH INSURANCE PRODUCTS

Introduction (Page 87)

✦ 1. The **price** of an insurance policy is the amount of the _____.

✦ 2. In insurance, **pricing** means setting _____.

3. The price of a policy must be set such that the policy is _____ but also such that the insurer can _____ and _____ or _____.

✦ 4. **Actuaries** are _____.

5. Both actuaries and underwriters are involved in pricing. In general, actuaries establish _____ and underwriters apply _____ _____.

The Four Principles of Insurance Pricing (Pages 87–88)

✦ 6. The four principles of insurance pricing are **adequacy, reasonableness, competitiveness**, and **equity.** Which principle is being violated in each of the following cases?

a. Evergreen Insurance charges a premium for its dental coverage that, while it is not particularly high considering the benefits provided by the coverage, is significantly higher that the premium charged by other companies for similar coverages.

b. Mid-State Insurance Company charges high premiums for its disability income insurance, such that what insureds receive in benefits is much less than what they pay in premiums.

c. Nova Insurance Company sets the premiums on its long-term care policies very low, such that what the company receives in premiums does not cover its costs.

d. Stateline Insurance Corporation charges some insureds less than the expected cost of providing coverage to them and charges others much more than cost.

7. If a premium amount for a policy is adequate, it covers _____ payments on the policy, _____ costs of the policy, and a reasonable amount of _____ or _____.

8. The difference between competitiveness and reasonableness is the following: a price is *reasonable* if it is a good price in terms of _____; a price is *competitive* if it is a good price in terms of _____.

9. If an insurer charges inadequate premiums, what will happen?

10. If the premiums for a policy are unreasonable, what will happen?

11. If an insurer charges more than its competitors, what will happen?

12. If an insurer does not charge each insured a premium amount that reflects (to the extent possible) the expected cost of providing coverage to that insured, what will happen?

The Components of a Premium Amount (Pages 88–89)

13. The amount of a premium is based on the estimated amounts of different kinds of _____, plus _____.

14. What are the six components of the necessary amount of a premium?

15. Which two of the six components are not cost components?

16. Five of the six components are added together to arrive at the necessary premium amount. Which component is subtracted? Why is this component subtracted?

17. Write the formula that expresses how the six components of a premium amount are combined.

18. The largest component of a premium amount is _____.

Claims (Pages 89–91)

19. In pricing, estimating claim costs means estimating the total amount of _____ that the insurer will make on the policy.

20. What are the two major factors that determine claim costs?

21. What two elements determine the two factors mentioned above?

♦ 22. Commonly, the term **morbidity** is used to mean _____.

♦ 23. Technically, **morbidity** is a number that expresses the amount of _____.

24. Morbidity is derived by multiplying two other numbers: _____ and _____.

♦ 25. **Frequency** is how often _____ occurs during _____, expressed as _____.

♦ 26. **Severity** is the _____.

27. Stylistics, Inc. has a group health insurance plan. For the group of those covered by the plan, there are on average two major surgical operations for every 100 individuals during a year. When someone in the group has such an operation, the average cost is $15,000. For a major surgical operation for this group, what is the frequency? What is the severity? What is the morbidity?

28. How does the average age of a group of people affect the morbidity of the group?

29. How does the proportion of males and females in a group of people affect the morbidity of the group?

30. (Higher-income / Lower-income) people tend to seek medical care more frequently and use more services.

31. How does income affect morbidity in disability income insurance?

32. How is morbidity affected by the industry the group members work in?

33. Normally, there is regional variation in (the cost of medical treatment but not the frequency or seriousness of illness and injury / the frequency or seriousness of illness and injury but not the cost of medical treatment / both the cost of medical treatment and the frequency and seriousness of illness and injury).

♦ 34. What is meant by the **level of participation** of a group?

35. How does the level of participation of a group affect the morbidity of the group?

36. In some cases, underwriting an individual is prohibited by law. How does this affect morbidity?

37. In some cases, underwriting of an individual is very thorough. How does this affect morbidity?

Reserves (Page 91)

38. Why is the number of claims *incurred* by a group during a period of time not usually the same as the number of claims *paid* during that period?

♦ 39. A claim incurred but not yet paid is known as an _____ claim.

♦ 40. An amount used by an actuary to cover the estimated amount of outstanding claims is a _____.

♦ 41. A claim reserve for claims that have been made, but that are being processed and have not yet been paid is known as a _____ claim reserve.

♦ 42. A claim reserve for losses that insureds have incurred but for which they have not yet submitted claims is known as an _____ claim reserve.

♦ 43. A **policy reserve** is used to account for (outstanding claims / future claims).

Margin (Pages 91–92)

♦ 44. Actuaries add an extra amount to the premium as a protection against the possibility that actual claims may be significantly higher than projected. This amount is known as a _____ margin or a _____ margin.

45. The amount of margin needed varies with the likelihood that _____.

46. How does each of these factors affect the amount of margin needed?

   a. The information on which claim projections are based.

   b. The size of a covered group.

   c. The period of time the premium rate is guaranteed.

Expenses (Pages 92–93)

✦ 47. In pricing, the term **expenses** normally refers to all costs not related to the money used for _____.

✦ 48. **Sales expenses** are costs associated with _____.

✦ 49. The most important sales expense is _____, and for this reason sales expenses are sometimes referred to as _____ expenses.

✦ 50. **Acquisition expenses** are costs related to the _____, _____ and _____ of policies.

✦ 51. **Maintenance expenses** are the costs of _____ and _____.

52. What are some of the activities the cost of which are included under maintenance expenses?

✦ 53. **General overhead expenses** are the costs of _____.

54. What are some of the costs included under general overhead expenses?

55. Premium taxes are levied by _____.

56. The premium of each policy must cover (only those expenses directly related to that policy / those expenses directly related to that policy and also a share of overall expenses).

✦ 57. Determining the amount of expenses that must be covered by a policy and included in the premium amount for that policy is known as _____ to the policy.

58. Explain the three main approaches to allocating expenses:

   a. Per policy.

   b. Percentage of premium.

   c. Percentage of claims.

59. For what kind of expenses is each of the three approaches to allocating expenses usually used?

    a. Per policy.

    b. Percentage of premium.

    c. Percentage of claims.

60. Expenses are normally higher in the first year of a policy than in later years because _____ expenses are incurred in the first year and sometimes _____ expenses are higher in the first year.

61. Why might sales expenses be higher in the first year of a policy?

62. An actuary sets (a higher premium rate for the first year and a lower rate for later years to account for higher first-year expenses / one amount such that first-year expenses are amortized over several years / either).

Profit (Pages 93–94)

63. A company's profits serve two purposes: a portion is paid to _____ as _____, and a portion is retained by the company for _____.

64. A company's surplus serves two purposes: to ensure that the company will be able to _____ even when _____ and to provide funds for _____.

65. Since a mutual company is not a profit-making enterprise, why does it need to bring in more money on a policy than just enough to cover its costs?

66. The amount an insurer can add to premium for profit is limited by _____ and in some cases by _____.

67. The contingency margin is intended to cover unusually high claims. If claims are not unusually high, what happens to the money not needed to cover claim payments?

68. What happens if claims are so high that the contingency margin is not sufficient to cover them?

♦ 69. Profit and expenses together make up the part of a premium amount that is not _____ but rather _____. Together they are referred to as _____.

Investment Income (Page 94)

70. Insurer investment income is derived from investing _____ and _____.

71. In calculating the amount of premium, investment income is (added / subtracted).

Answers

1. Premium.

2. The premium amount.

3. Advantageous and attractive to the insured; cover its costs and make a profit or add to surplus.

4. Insurance mathematicians.

5. An insurer's pricing formulas; these formulas to particular cases.

6. a. Competitiveness.

   b. Reasonableness.

   c. Adequacy.

   d. Equity.

7. Benefit; administrative; profit or contribution to surplus.

8. The benefits it buys; the prices of similar products offered by others.

9. It may sell a lot of policies, but it will not make a profit and may even lose money on those policies.

10. People will feel that the coverage provided is not worth the amount charged and will not buy the policies.

11. Few people will buy its policies.

12. If the insurer charges some insureds less than cost, it will have to charge other insureds an extra amount to make up for this loss. Those paying extra will go to other insurers, leaving the insurer with only those insureds paying less than cost.

13. Costs; profit.

14. Claims, reserves, margin, expenses, profit, and investment income.

15. Profit and investment income.

16. Investment income. It is not a cost that the premium must cover but rather a financial gain that partially offsets the need for premium payments.

17. Claims + Reserves + Margin + Expenses + Profit − Investment Income = Premium Amount

19. Claims.

19. Benefit payments.

20. • What kinds of losses the insurer must pay benefits for and what amounts it must pay for various losses.

    • How often insureds will incur covered losses and how severe those losses will be.

21. The provisions of the policy and the morbidity of the people insured.

22. The likelihood of injury or illness.

23. Financial loss that a certain group of people is likely to incur over a certain period of time.

24. Frequency and severity.

25. A loss; a year; a percentage.

26. Average amount of loss.

27. 2 percent; $15,000; $300.

28. Older people have more frequent and more serious health problems than younger people, so a higher average age usually means greater morbidity.

29. At most ages, women have more health problems on average than men, so a group with more women will usually have greater morbidity.

30. Higher-income.

31. The amount of benefits is directly based on the income level of the insured.

32. Those working in some industries have more frequent and more serious injuries than those in other fields and more frequent and longer periods of disability.

33. The cost of medical treatment but not the frequency or seriousness of illness and injury.

34. The percentage of the eligible members of a group who take coverage.

35. When participation is low, there is a greater chance of adverse selection (that is, a greater likelihood that people with health problems will disproportionately choose coverage and make the morbidity of the group higher than it would normally be).

36. Adverse selection often occurs, making morbidity higher than average.

37. Usually any current serious illness is detected, making morbidity lower than average during the first years of the policy.

38. A claim is paid some time after a loss occurs, so for any period there are always a significant number of claims that were incurred during the period but not paid until later.

39. Outstanding.

40. Claim reserve.

41. Pending.

42. Incurred but not reported (IBNR).

43. Future claims.

44. Contingency; morbidity fluctuation.

45. Actual claims will be higher than projected.

46. a. If information is limited or not considered completely reliable, unexpectedly high claims are more   probable and the amount of margin must be greater.

  b. The larger the group, the smaller the fluctuation in claims and the less likely are unexpectedly high claims. Thus, the larger the group, the smaller the margin.

  c. The longer the period, the more difficult accurate prediction is, and the greater the margin must be.

47. Paying claims.

48. The solicitation of new business.

49. Sales commissions to agents and brokers; sales compensation.

50. Underwriting, issuance, and installation.

51. Administering a policy and processing claims.

52. Maintaining records, billing and collecting premiums, processing claims, and other activities.

53. Running a business.

54. The costs of physical plant, office furniture and equipment, recruiting and training, and the salaries of executives.

55. Each state.

56. Those expenses directly related to that policy and also a share of overall expenses.

57. Allocating expenses.

58. a. Expenses are divided equally among all policies.

  b. Expenses are allocated to each policy according to the amount of premium.

  c. Expenses are allocated according to the amount of claims expected to be paid on a policy.

59. a. For expenses that are roughly the same for each policy (such as underwriting and issuance).

  b. For expenses (such as sales commissions and premium taxes) that are directly determined by the amount of premium charged for a policy.

  c. For claim administration expenses.

60. Acquisition; sales.

61. A high-low commission schedule may be used or sales bonuses paid.

62. One amount such that first-year expenses are amortized over several years.

63. Stockholders as a return on their investment; addition to surplus.

64. Pay claims and otherwise meet its obligations even when the insurer's costs exceed its income; growth and development projects.

65. It must add to its surplus, which it needs to guarantee its obligations and to fund growth and development.

66. The principles of pricing; regulations.

67. It can be added to profits.

68. Funds must be taken from profits to pay them.

69. Returned to insureds in the form of benefits; retained by the insurer for its purposes; retention.

70. Cash flow and reserve funds.

71. Subtracted.

14 THE PRICING PROCESS

Introduction (Page 97)

◆ 1. A premium rate is _____.

◆ 2. A premium is _____.

◆ 3. Per unit of coverage can mean per _____ or per _____

4. For group health insurance plans, the premium amount usually is obtained by multiplying the _____ by the _____.

5. Midwest State University has a group health insurance plan, for which it pays an insurer $80 per employee per month. Last month, Midwest had exactly 400 employees covered by the plan. What was the premium rate that month? What was the premium?

6. In individual insurance, the premium rate and the premium are often the same; that is, _____.

◆ 7. Another term for pricing is _____.

Group Rating Methods (Pages 97–100)

◆ 8. In experience rating, a group's premium rates are based on _____, which are based on _____.

◆ 9. In manual rating, a group's premium rates are based on _____, which are based on _____.

◆ 10. A combination of the above two approaches is known as _____.

11. Why is experience rating used only for large groups?

12. Why must manual rating be used for small groups?

13. Why is the blended approach taken for some medium-size groups?

14. How does the type of coverage help determine whether there is a large enough body of claim data for experience rating?

15. In rating one group, (the same method must be used for all coverages / different methods may be used for different coverages).

◆ 16. To determine the level of past claims, an actuary must choose a sample period of time, known as the _____ period.

17. The experience period must be at least 12 months to eliminate _____.

18. What is the advantage of using the most recent 12-month period as the experience period?

19. What is the advantage of using the last several years as the experience period?

20. How do some insurers combine both approaches?

21. An actuary projects future claims based on the amount of _____ during _____.

22. Describe how incurred claims for a period are calculated.

♦ 23. Estimated amounts for outstanding claims are known as _____.

24. An actuary might make adjustments in premium amounts to reflect recent changes. Give some examples of such changes.

25. After the projection of future claims is finalized, the actuary calculates the premium rate by adding amounts for _____, _____, and _____ and subtracting an amount for _____.

26. The rates in a rating manual for a given coverage are based on the average _____.

27. Intercompany studies contain claim data from _____.

28. Intercompany studies are used by insurers that _____.

29. Intercompany studies are produced by_____, _____, and _____.

30. A rating manual contains a range of possible premium rates for a given coverage. The rates differ according to different _____ and different _____ such as _____, _____, _____, _____, and _____.

31. Manual rating involves matching _____ and _____ to the proper rate.

32. The rates in rating manuals are based on claim costs only, not the other components of a premium amount, because the other components involve more _____ than can be incorporated into a manual.

33. Since the non-claim components of a premium amount are not included in manual rates, how are they reflected in the premium?

34. Why do actuaries sometimes adjust manual rates downward for larger groups and upward for smaller groups?

35. In what circumstances may an actuary blend actual experience with manual rates?

36. Treasury Manufacturing has a group health insurance plan. In rating this group, an actuary assigns it a credibility percentage of 75. This means the premium will be based (75 / 25) percent on the group's experience and (75 / 25) percent on manual rates.

37. In the above example, Treasury's group is probably (medium-large / medium-small).

Rating Individual Policies (Pages 100–101)

38. Individual pricing is similar to small group pricing: Premium rates are based on rates from _____, which are based on _____.

39. In individual pricing, as in small group pricing, actuaries usually match _____ and _____ to the proper premium in the manual and make adjustments for the other _____.

♦ 40. In some cases, insurers use the same premium rates for all policies providing the same coverage—that is, rates are the same for all persons, regardless of such characteristics as age, sex, and occupation. This is known as _____ rating.

41. The rating method described above is sometimes required by _____.

42. In an individual policy, the level of claims almost always increases during the life of the policy because the insured is _____.

43. In a group policy, the level of claims does not usually increase during the life of the plan. Why not?

♦ 44. In some individual policies, rates go up automatically as the insured ages. This is known as _____ rating.

♦ 45. In some individual policies, rates do not go up with age. This is known as _____ rating.

♦ 46. In some individual policies, rates do not go up with age, but an individual's rate depends in part on her age when she first bought the policy. (Those who buy when they are young get better rates than those who buy when they are older.) This is known as _____ rating.

47. In attained-age rating, rates may increase (each year / when the insured moves from one age band to another / either, depending on the policy).

48. How does level rating address the problem of increasing claims as the insured ages?

♦ 49. A reserve used to pay benefits in the later years of a policy is known as a _____ reserve or an _____ reserve.

50. Entry-age rating is a form of (attained-age / level) rating.

51. (Level / Attained-age) rating is more complicated. Why?

52. What disadvantage does attained-age rating have?

Rerating (Pages 101–102)

53. For medical expense coverage and most group coverages, initial rates are usually guaranteed for (six months / 12 months / two years).

54. After an initial period of guaranteed rates, insurers may generally reset rates (at any time / at set intervals / on any premium due date / at set intervals or any premium due date, depending on the policy).

55. Insurers most commonly rerate every (six months / year / two years).

56. Rate changes are most commonly effective on _____.

57. The main difference between rating and rerating is that, in rerating, actuaries do not start at zero in making predictions, but rather review _____ and compare them to _____.

58. An insurer must usually notify a policyholder of a rate change at least (30 days / 60 days / six months) in advance.

59. Generally, when an insurer is rerating at the end of the first year of coverage, it can make a rate change effective on the first anniversary date or a few months after that date. What is the disadvantage of making the change effective on the first anniversary date?

60. What is the advantage of making a rate change effective a few months after the first anniversary date?

61. An insurer usually prefers to make a rate change effective (on the first anniversary date, despite having to base rerating on less than a year's experience / after the first anniversary date, so that it can be based on a year's experience).

62. An insurer is more likely to make rate changes effective on the first anniversary date instead of later if there are indications that claims are _____.

63. When proposing a rate increase, some insurers also offer alternatives without rate increases. How do these alternatives avoid rate increases?

64. Normally, when an insurer provides a package of several coverages to an individual or group, (each separate coverage is profitable / the whole package is profitable, but each separate coverage may not be).

65. In rerating a package of several coverages, (each separate coverage must be kept profitable / sometimes a coverage may be allowed to become unprofitable, as long as the whole package remains profitable).

◆ 66. How does an **experience refund** work?

67. Experience refunds are required by some (individual / small group / large group) policies.

68. Rerating and the experience refund determination process both analyze claim data, but their goals differ. The purpose of rerating is to_____. The purpose of experience refund determination is to find differences between _____ and_____ so that any difference can be_____.

The Regulation of Pricing (Page 103)

69. Insurers often must submit premium rates to _____ for review and approval.

♦ 70. Regulators often look at a policy's **loss ratio**, which is the proportion of premium payments that is _____.

♦ 71. What does a **mandated benefit** require?

72. Some states prohibit or limit basing premium rates for individuals on an individual's _____, _____, or _____.

♦ 73. **Small group reform legislation** regulates health insurance policies for groups of _____ full-time permanent employees.

74. What limitations on pricing do small group reform laws commonly impose in these areas?

   a. Different rates for different small groups.

   b. Rate increases.

   c. Rates for individual members of group plans.

Summary (Page 103)

75. The most important part of the process of pricing a policy is predicting the amount of _____.

76. For large groups, this prediction is usually based on _____.

77. For small groups and individuals, this prediction is based on _____.

78. What approach is taken for some medium-size groups?

Answers

1. An amount charged per unit of coverage.

2. The total amount charged the policyholder for coverage.

3. Person; dollar amount of benefit.

4. Premium rate by the number of covered employees.

5. The premium rate was $80; the monthly premium was $32,000.

6. The amount charged per policy.

7. Rating.

8. Claim projections for the group; the benefits paid to members of the group in the past.

9. Standard rates from the insurer's rating manual; averages of the benefit payments made in the past to many groups.

10. Blended manual/experience rating.

11. Only a large group has a body of claim experience data large enough to be a reliable basis for the prediction of future claims.

12. The claim data of a small group is not large enough to be a reliable predictor of future claims, so actuaries use another large body of data-the averages of the claim experience of many groups, contained in the insurer's rating manual.

13. The claim experience of medium-size groups is large enough to be somewhat but not completely reliable, so both manual rates and experience are used.

14. Some coverages (such as medical expense insurance) involve many claims and consequently produce a large body of data, while for other coverages (such as disability income insurance) claims are relatively infrequent.

15. Different methods may be used for different coverages.

16. Experience.

17. Seasonal variations in illness.

18. This period reflects recent changes.

19. Several years are more likely to be typical than a single year.

20. They use several years but give more weight to recent experience.

21. Incurred claims; the experience period.

22. Begin with claims paid during the period. Subtract claims paid during the period but incurred before the period began. Add estimated amounts for covered losses that occurred during the period for which claims have not yet been submitted, or for which claims have been submitted but not yet paid.

23. Claim reserves.

24. Changes in group characteristics (such as age and income), in health care costs, in the general business environment (which may affect expenses and investment income), and in the benefits provided to the group.

25. Contingency margin, expenses, and profit; investment income.

26. Claim experience of a large number of groups with that coverage.

27. Groups of many insurers.

28. Do not have enough claim data from their own groups to produce a manual.

29. The Society of Actuaries, other professional organizations, and private consulting firms.

30. Benefits provisions; group characteristics such as age, sex, geographic location, income, and industry.

31. The benefit package being offered and the characteristics of the group being insured.

32. Variables.

33. Actuaries adjust manual rates to reflect the non-claim components.

34. Smaller groups have higher-than-average expenses per insured person, and larger groups have lower-than-average expenses.

35. If a group's body of claim experience data is not large enough for full experience rating, but it is large enough that taking it into account will make the estimate of future claims more accurate.

36. 75; 25.

37. Medium-large.

38. Rating manuals; the claim experience of a large number of individuals with the same or a similar policy.

39. The benefits provided and the insured's characteristics (age, sex, occupation, etc.); premium components.

40. Community.

41. State insurance law.

42. Aging.

43. As older workers retire and younger workers are hired, the average age of the group tends to remain relatively stable.

44. Attained-age.

45. Level.

46. Entry-age.

47. Either, depending on the policy.

48. Rates are set such that during the early years of the policy the insurer makes more than enough to cover costs. This extra money is put into a reserve and invested, and the earnings are used to pay benefits in the later years of the policy, when claims exceed premiums.

49. Policy reserve or active life reserve.

50. Level.

51. Level. Rates must be set such that claims and premiums balance out over a long period of time.

52. Continually rising rates tend to discourage insureds from continuing coverage.

53. 12 months.

54. At set intervals or any premium due date, depending on the policy.

55. Year.

56. The anniversary of the effective date of the policy.

57. Previous projections; actual experience.

58. 30 days.

59. Because rerating takes time, it must begin a few months before the date it goes into effect. Therefore, if a change goes into effect at the anniversary date, rerating will be based on less than a year's claim experience.

60. Rerating can be based on a full year of claim experience, which is more reliable.

61. After the first anniversary date, so that it can be based on a year's experience.

62. Higher than expected.

63. They reduce claims by reducing benefits, increasing deductibles or coinsurance, or introducing managed care features.

64. Each separate coverage is profitable.

65. Sometimes a coverage may be allowed to become unprofitable, as long as the whole package remains profitable.

66. If the cost of providing coverage turns out to be less than the insurer projected, the insurer must refund a portion of premium payments to the policyholder.

67. Large group.

68. Project future claims; claims for a recent period and the projections made for that period; reimbursed to the policyholder.

69. State insurance departments.

70. Returned to insureds in the form of benefit payments.

71. That all policies of a certain type cover certain medical services.

72. Age, sex, or occupation.

73. Two to 25 (or sometimes two to 50).

74. a. There are limits to the extent to which different groups may be charged different rates based on group characteristics.

    b. The amount of rate increases for small groups are limited.

    c. No individual member of a small group can be charged a different premium rate based on her medical history.

75. Claim payments that the insurer will make on the policy.

76. The past claims of the group.

77. Averages of the claims of other groups and individuals, contained in rating manuals.

78. A blend of the above two approaches.

15 THE REGULATION OF INSURANCE

Why Is Insurance Regulated? (Page 106)

1. The insurance industry is highly regulated, in part because of the issues of _____ and _____.

2. In most business transactions, one party pays money to another party and in return receives _____ from that party.

3. In an insurance transaction, the policyholder pays premiums to the insurer and in return receives _____.

4. The solvency of an insurer is important to the policyholder because if the insurer is not solvent, it will not be able to _____.

5. Why do government regulators take responsibility for verifying and ensuring the solvency of insurers?

6. Insurance contracts are different from some other kinds of contracts in that one party to the contract, the insurer, has _____, while the other party, the policyholder, usually does not.

7. Governments establish standards of fairness and require that all insurance contracts meet them because policyholders do not usually have _____.

◆ 8. A **fiduciary organization** is a business that _____, such as _____, _____, and _____.

The Regulatory Environment of Insurance (Pages 107–109)

9. Before 1944, regulation of insurance was handled by the (states / federal government).

10. In 1944, the U.S. Supreme Court ruled that insurance is interstate commerce, which the Constitution gives the (states / federal government) the right to regulate.

11. In the McCarran-Ferguson Act of 1945, Congress decided to (stop states from regulating insurance and begin regulating this area itself / allow states to continue regulating insurance and give up its constitutional right to regulate in this area / allow the states to continue regulating insurance without giving up its right to legislate in this area).

12. The insurance industry is regulated (primarily by the states with some federal involvement / equally by the states and the federal government / primarily by the federal government with some state involvement).

13. In recent years, the federal role in the regulation of insurance has (increased / decreased / remained about the same).

◆ 14. In most states, insurance laws are grouped together in what is known as the _____.

◆ 15. A **state insurance department** is an agency of the executive branch of each state government that has responsibility for _____.

◆ 16. State insurance departments issue rules that specify what insurers, agents, and others must do to comply with the laws. These rules are known as _____.

◆ 17. State insurance departments publish bulletins, guidelines, and official letters that clarify laws and official regulations. These documents are sometimes referred to as _____ or _____.

18. Laws are _____ by a _____; regulations are _____ by a _____.

19. The National Association of Insurance Commissioners (NAIC) is made up of the heads of _____.

20. When the NAIC proposes a model law, states have a number of options. Which of the following actions can a state legislature take? (Adopting it without change / adopting it in part / adopting a modified version of it / not adopting it at all).

21. Which statement is the most accurate description of the impact of NAIC model laws on state insurance laws and regulations?

- All states have adopted most NAIC model laws with few changes, so that there is a high degree of uniformity in state laws and regulations.

- In general, states have adopted some NAIC model laws, modified some, and rejected some, so that there are both differences and similarities in state laws and regulations.

- Most states have enacted few NAIC model laws, so that there is little uniformity in state laws and regulations.

22. State A has more insurance laws than State B, but the regulation of insurance is actually stricter in State B. How is this possible?

◆ 23. The state of South Caledonia has some laws that are **extraterritorial**. If Jupiter Insurance Company, headquartered in the state of North Caledonia, sells a policy to a resident of South Caledonia, the policy will be subject to (all the laws of North Caledonia and none of the laws of South Caledonia / the extraterritorial laws of South Caledonia and none of the laws of North Caledonia / all the laws of North Caledonia and the extraterritorial laws of South Caledonia / all the laws of North Caledonia and all the laws of South Caledonia).

24. Federal insurance laws are administered and enforced by (the U.S. Department of Insurance / various agencies of the executive branch of the federal government).

25. In insurance as in other fields, court decisions create _____ that determine how laws and regulations are _____ and how contracts are _____.

26. Give some example of the sorts of decisions that courts make in the insurance field.

Insurer Compliance with Laws and Regulations
(Pages 109–110)

✦ 27. **Regulatory compliance** consists of the actions taken by insurance company personnel to ensure that the company _____.

✦ 28. In some companies, regulatory compliance is the responsibility of a body of representatives of various areas of the company, known as a _____.

✦ 29. In some companies, a staff of persons is hired to handle compliance. This staff is known as a _____.

30. A large company is most likely to have a compliance (committee / division).

31. The role of an insurance company's legal department in compliance is to _____ and sometimes to monitor _____.

32. What role do industry associations like America's Health Insurance Plans (AHIP) play in the area of compliance?

Answers

1. Solvency; contracts.

2. A good or service.

3. The insurer's promise that if she suffers a covered loss, the insurer will pay her a benefit.

4. Pay benefits.

5. Because policyholders do not normally have the resources and skills needed to do this.

6. Expertise in these contracts.

7. The knowledge needed to determine if a contract is reasonable and fair.

8. Holds money in trust for others; insurers, banks, and trust companies.

9. States.

10. Federal government.

11. Allow the states to continue regulating insurance without giving up its right to legislate in this area.

12. Primarily by the states with some federal involvement.

13. Increased.

14. Insurance code.

15. Administering and enforcing the insurance laws passed by the legislature.

16. Official regulations.

17. Informal regulations; regulatory guidance.

18. Enacted by a legislature; issued by a government agency.

19. The state insurance departments.

20. A state can take any of these actions.

21. In general, states have adopted some NAIC model laws, modified some, and rejected some, so that there are both differences and similarities in state laws and regulations.

22. State B has few laws but extensive regulations.

23. All the laws of North Caledonia and the extraterritorial laws of South Caledonia.

24. Various agencies of the executive branch of the federal government.

25. Judicial precedents; applied; interpreted.

26. A court may decide precisely what actions are permitted and forbidden by a law or regulation, or whether a regulation issued by a government agency is consistent with relevant laws, or what the language of a contract means.

27. Fulfills the requirements of all state and federal laws and regulations.

28. Compliance committee.

29. Compliance division.

30. Division.

31. Render opinions on the meaning of laws, regulations, or court decisions; changes in regulation.

32. They follow developments in the regulatory environment and publish bulletins informing insurers of possible or actual changes.

16 STATE REGULATION OF HEALTH INSURANCE

Areas Addressed by State Health Insurance Laws and Regulations (Pages 111–113)

1. Give a few examples of laws and regulations affecting policy provisions.

✦ 2. What are **mandated benefits** (or **mandates**)?

3. Mandated benefits are becoming (more / less) common.

4. In the past, mandated benefits generally pertained only to (group / individual) insurance, but increasingly they apply to (group / individual) policies as well.

5. States seek to guarantee insurer solvency principally by requiring insurers to maintain _____ and by restricting insurers' _____.

6. Typically, state laws require _____ of insurer investments, and they limit investments that _____.

7. In the area of claims, state laws prohibit various actions by insurers. List four of these.

8. Name four insurer actions in claim processing for which states often establish time limits.

9. In an increasing number of states, if an insurer does not pay an amount due to a claimant within a specified number of days, the insurer must _____.

10. In regulating premium rates, states usually require a balance between _____ and _____.

✦ 11. How does **guaranteed issue** work?

12. State laws governing the advertising of health insurance try to ensure that advertisements are _____ and not _____.

13. What do state laws usually require advertisements for health insurance to disclose?

14. The readability of the language of an insurance policy usually refers to whether _____ can understand it.

15. Laws establish standards for the way personal information may be _____ in connection with insurance transactions and how this information can be _____ and _____.

16. In addition to ethnicity, religion, sex, or age, some state laws also prohibit discrimination based on other criteria. What are some of these?

Administering and Enforcing State Insurance Law: The State Insurance Department (Pages 113–117)

17. A few states do not have a state insurance department, but rather a department that handles the regulation of both _____ and _____ or the regulation of all _____.

♦ 18. The head of a state insurance department is usually called the_____.

19. How is a state insurance commissioner most commonly placed in office?

20. Although the state insurance department is part of the executive branch of government, the legislature also has certain powers over it. What are they?

21. In order to do business in most states, an (insurance company / insurance agent / both) needs a license granted by the state insurance department of that state.

22. How does a state insurance department's right to withhold or withdraw an insurer's or an agent's license give the department great power over insurers and agents?

23. Under what circumstances would an insurance department withhold or withdraw a license from an insurer or agent?

24. To obtain an insurance agent's license, a person must _____, or, in some states, she must _____.

25. Licenses are most commonly (permanent / annually renewable).

26. Most states require as a condition of license renewal that agents submit proof that they have _____.

♦ 27. The laws of most states require that before an insurer can issue a policy in the state, the insurer must **file the policy.** What does this mean?

28. Filing a policy is required so that regulators can verify that it meets three basic criteria. What are they?

29. What happens if a policy does not meet the above-mentioned criteria?

30. The filing of premium rates enables a state insurance department to confirm that the premium charged is _____.

31. Most states require insurers to file (no / some / all) rates for individual health insurance policies.

32. Some states require insurers selling group insurance to file _____ _____.

♦ 33. In some cases, insurers cannot charge a rate until it has been approved. This approach is known as _____.

♦ 34. In some cases, insurers can begin charging a rate as soon as they have filed it, without waiting for approval. This approach is known as _____.

35. For both group and individual health insurance, some states require an actuarial memorandum showing how _____ and indicating the anticipated _____. For individual insurance, insurers may have to file the actual _____ for each year.

♦ 36. What is a **loss ratio**?

37. What type of information is included in the annual statements submitted by insurers to the state insurance department?

38. The information in an insurer's annual report is used by the state insurance department to confirm that _____.

39. If an insurance company becomes insolvent or is in danger of doing so, the state insurance department (may withdraw the insurer's license, but may not directly involve itself in the management of the company / may take over the company).

40. If an insurer has become insolvent, the state insurance department's first step is normally (to try to restore the company's solvency / to liquidate the company).

41. If an insurer becomes insolvent and is liquidated, what happens to its policies?

42. State insurance departments conduct examinations of insurance companies to verify that _____ and that _____.

43. State insurance departments usually examine insurers every (six months / year / three to five years).

44. A state insurance department has the right to examine any insurer (headquartered in / operating in) that state.

45. Most commonly, the examination of an insurer is conducted (by the state where it is headquartered only / by all states where it operates, acting separately / by all states where it operates, working together).

46. What is involved in the examination of an insurer?

47. Which of these do insurance inspectors have the right to do? (Inspect a company's records / interrogate a company's officers / interrogate a company's agents and employees).

48. The cost of the examination of an insurer is paid for by (license fees paid by all insurers / premium taxes paid by all insurers / the insurer being examined).

♦ 49. A **market conduct examination** focuses on how a company behaves toward (competitors / consumers).

50. What parts of a company's operations does a market conduct examination look at?

51. What are the most common complaints in the following areas?

    a. Claim administration.

    b. Underwriting.

    c. Sales.

52. If it receives a complaint about an insurer, a state insurance department's first step is usually to contact _____.

53. If an insurer or agent violates the laws and regulations of a state, the most common penalty is _____.

54. License revocation is rarely used, (so it does not have much impact on ensuring compliance with laws and regulations / but because of its severity, the threat of its use has a great impact on ensuring compliance with laws and regulations.

55. If an insurer or agent is found guilty of a violation, in addition to the penalties imposed by the state where the violation occurred, what other negative consequences may there be?

State Taxes and Fees (Page 117)

56. (No / Some / All) states impose a premium tax on insurers headquartered in the state.

57. (No / Some / All) states impose a premium tax on insurers headquartered out of the state but operating in the state.

58. Insurers headquartered (in a state / outside a state) usually pay a lower premium tax rate to that state.

59. Insurers often charge insurers fees for the privilege of _____ and for many of the transactions involved in administering insurance regulation, such as _____, _____, and _____.

Summary (Page 118)

60. List the main areas of health insurance addressed by state laws and regulations.

61. List the ways state insurance departments determine whether insurers and agents are in compliance with state laws and regulations.

Answers

1. Laws requiring provisions that give policyholders certain rights of renewal or reinstatement, provisions that limit the insurer's right to contest a policy, and provisions that provide benefits for certain expenses.

2. Benefit provisions that are required by law.

3. More.

4. Group; individual.

5. Financial reserves; investments.

6. Diversification; tend to fluctuate greatly in value.

7. • Misrepresenting the facts of a case or the provisions of a policy;

   • refusing to pay a claim without conducting a reasonable investigation based on all available information;

   • refusing to explain the reason for denying a claim; and

   • forcing the insured to start legal action to collect an amount due.

8. Acknowledging a claim, furnishing claim forms, answering a claimant's correspondence, and paying or denying a claim.

9. Pay the claimant interest.

10. Benefits and premiums.

11. Any insurer selling to a certain market (for example, small groups) must accept any applicant that meets certain basic eligibility requirements.

12. Truthful; not misleading.

13. Exceptions, limitations, and policy provisions relating to renewability, cancelability, and termination.

14. An average consumer.

15. Obtained; used and disclosed.

16. Marital status, sexual orientation, deafness, blindness, visual acuity, lawful occupation, or the presence of certain genetic traits (such as sickle cell and Tay-Sachs diseases).

17. Insurance and banking; business.

18. Insurance commissioner.

19. She is appointed by the governor and confirmed by the legislature.

20. The legislature enacts the laws that the insurance department enforces and that govern its operation, and it controls the department's budget.

21. Both.

22. An insurer or agent cannot sell insurance in the state without a license.

23. If the department determines that the operations of the insurer or agent are not in compliance with the law or are in some other way unsatisfactory (as when a company's solvency is questionable).

24. Pass a written examination; complete an approved course of study.

25. Annually renewable.

26. Earned continuing education units (CEUs).

27. The insurer must submit the policy to the state insurance department for prior approval,

28. • The policy complies with all state laws and regulations.

   • The terms of the policy are fair to the insured.

   • The language of the policy is clear, unambiguous, consistent, and not misleading in any way.

29. The insurance department will not approve the policy, and it cannot be used in the state.

30. Reasonable in relation to the benefits provided.

31. All.

32. Their standard first-year group rates from their rating manuals.

33. File for approval.

34. File and use.

35. Rates were developed; loss ratio; loss ratios.

36. The proportion of premium payments returned to the insured as benefit payments.

37. The insurer's financial condition and its financial results for the year, as well as information on the insurer's assets, liabilities, reserves, surplus, investments, income, operating costs, and other matters.

38. The insurer is solvent.

39. May take over the company.

40. To try to restore the company's solvency.

41. The state insurance department tries to find a solvent company to take them over.

42. Their practices are in compliance with state laws and regulations and that they are financially stable.

43. Three to five years.

44. Operating in.

45. By the state where it is headquartered only.

46. A visit to the company and a review of the company's operation.

47. All of these.

48. The insurer being examined.

49. Consumers.

50. Sales and marketing activities, underwriting and rating practices, claim administration, policyholder service, and complaint handling.

51. a. Insureds usually believe a claim that was denied should have been paid.

   b. Complaints commonly involve a dispute as to the individual's insurability.

   c. Complaints involve improper methods used by an agent.

52. The insurer.

53. A fine.

54. Because of its severity, the threat of its use has a great impact on ensuring compliance with laws and regulations.

55. The insurer or agent is often subject to closer scrutiny by regulators. That is, examinations may be done more frequently, and policies and reports may be looked at more carefully. This may occur not only in the state where the violation occurred but in other states as well.

56. Some.

57. All.

58. In a state.

59. Doing business in the state; licensing insurers and agents, filing policies, and filing financial statements.

60. Policy provisions, solvency, claim administration, premium rates, availability of coverage, agents and brokers, advertising, readability, personal information, and discrimination.

61. Conducting examinations of insurers, reviewing policies and premium rates, reviewing insurer financial reports, and investigating complaints.

17 FEDERAL GOVERNMENT INVOLVEMENT IN HEALTH INSURANCE

Introduction (Page 119)

1. The federal government impacts the health insurance industry in two main ways. What are they?

Major Federal Legislation Affecting Health Insurance (Pages 119–122)

2. ERISA stands for the _____.

3. The principal purpose of ERISA is to regulate _____ in order to protect the interests of _____.

4. ERISA affects health insurance because it also regulates _____, including _____.

✦ 5. A **summary plan description** is a document that informs participants in a group benefit plan of their _____ and _____ under the plan.

6. If a group health insurance plan covers more than 100 persons, the employer must (submit the summary plan description / make the summary plan description available on request) to the U.S. Department of Labor.

✦ 7. A **fiduciary** of a benefit plan is a person who has the authority to _____ _____ and the obligation to _____.

8. Under ERISA, when an employee benefit plan denies a participant's claim, it must give _____, and the participant must have the right to have his claim _____.

9. The preemption provision of ERISA states that because ERISA imposes federal regulations on employers sponsoring benefit plans, these employers are exempt from _____.

10. In general, the courts have (confirmed / denied) the right of states to regulate plan sponsors in cases where ERISA applies.

11. ERISA exempts (employers only / insurers only / both) from state laws intended to regulate their management of benefit plans.

12. HIPAA stands for the _____.

13. The purpose of HIPAA is to _____.

14. HIPAA was enacted in (1976 / 1986 / 1996).

15. HIPAA represented a major change in the regulatory environment because it was the first major federal law that (affected health insurance / regulated health insurers).

16. HIPAA marked a shift away from Congress's previous approach to the regulation of health insurance, which was to

17. How does HIPAA attempt to ensure that people who have lost their group coverage because they have changed or lost their jobs can obtain new coverage?

18. HIPAA limits the exclusions of preexisting conditions in several ways in (group / individual / both group and individual) health insurance policies.

19. What does HIPAA require of insurers selling to the small group market in terms of the acceptance of groups and individuals?

20. Except in a few specified circumstances, HIPAA requires insurers to renew (group / individual / both group and individual) policies for (medical expense coverage only / both medical expense and disability income coverages / all health coverages).

21. COBRA stands for the _____.

22. COBRA applies to employers with (20 / 50 / 100) or more employees.

23. COBRA requires employers to allow continuation of group health care coverage for (6 / 12 / 18) months, for (employees only / employees and their dependents), at the (employer's / employee's) expense.

24. FMLA stands for the _____.

25. FMLA gives eligible employees the right to take up to (6 / 12 / 26) work weeks of unpaid leave during a period of (6 / 12 / 24) months.

26. Under FMLA, what are the reasons for which an employee may take leave?

27. How does FMLA affect health insurance?

28. How does Title Seven of the Civil Rights Act of 1964 affect health insurance?

29. A 1978 amendment to Title Seven of the Civil Rights Act requires employers to treat _____, for all employment-related purposes, the same as any other medical condition.

30. The provisions of the 1978 amendment to Title Seven of the Civil Rights Act concerning pregnancy apply to the payment of benefits for (medical expense insurance but not disability income insurance / both medical expense insurance and disability income insurance).

31. The 1978 amendment to Title Seven of the Civil Rights Act has been interpreted to mean that dependent wives (must / need not) receive the same pregnancy benefits as female employees.

32. The Age Discrimination in Employment Act (ADEA) prohibits employers with (20 / 50 / 100) or more employees from discriminating against individuals aged (40 / 60 / 65) or older in all aspects of employment, including employee benefits.

33. The Age Discrimination in Employment Act allows for a reduction in disability benefits for older employees, provided the employer spends _____ _____.

34. How does the Americans with Disabilities Act (ADA) affect health insurance?

35. The Fair Credit Reporting Act regulates organizations involved in gathering, using, and reporting information on individuals in the areas of _____, _____, and _____.

36. The Fair Credit Reporting Act requires that organizations using personal information adopt reasonable procedures to ensure four things. What are they?

Federal Health Care Benefit Programs (Pages 123–125)

37. The Medicare program pays benefits for health care expenses of persons _____ and _____.

38. Medicare Part A, Part B, or both?

    a. Received by all Medicare beneficiaries.

    b. Optional program.

    c. Beneficiaries do not pay premiums.

    d. Beneficiaries pay a portion of premiums.

    e. Provides benefits for hospital care, skilled nursing care, home health services, hospice care, and blood.

    f. Requires the payment of deductibles and coinsurance.

39. For what expenses does Medicare Part B pay benefits?

40. What purpose does Medicare supplement insurance serve?

41. How does Medicare often affect dependent coverage in group policies?

42. Federal laws make the Medicare program the secondary payer to employers' group health plans in certain circumstances. This means that the group plan pays _____ and Medicare pays for _____.

43. The Medicaid program pays benefits for health care expenses of _____.

44. What are the roles of the federal government and state governments in Medicaid?

45. The federal government requires that state Medicaid programs provide benefits to all of those (below a certain income level / who qualify for public assistance). State programs (may not provide Medicaid benefits to anyone else / must provide benefits to anyone else determined to be medically needy / may provide benefits to others determined to be medically needy, but are not required to do so).

46. List the areas in which the federal government requires state Medicaid programs to provide a minimal level of benefits.

47. State Medicaid programs may not require cost sharing except under two conditions. What are they?

48. The TRICARE program pays benefits for health care expenses of _____.

49. Those receiving TRICARE benefits include _____, _____, and _____.

50. John Ukridge is a 70-year-old retiree from the Air Force. He receives medical benefits from (TRICARE / Medicare).

51. TRICARE replaced a similar program called _____.

52. Since the government directly provides health care services to those associated with the uniformed services in military hospitals and clinics, why is TRICARE needed?

53. What purpose does TRICARE supplement insurance serve?

Answers

1. • Congress enacts laws that affect health insurance.

   • Federal government programs provide health care benefits to certain classes of people.

2. Employee Retirement Income Security Act.

3. Employer-sponsored pension plans; employees participating in them.

4. Employer-sponsored benefit plans, including group health insurance plans.

5. Rights and obligations.

6. Make the summary plan description available on request.

7. Manage the operation of the plan; act in the interest of the participants.

8. An adequate explanation; reviewed by the plan's fiduciary.

9. Any state laws intended to regulate their involvement in these plans.

10. Denied.

11. Employers only.

12. Health Insurance Portability and Accountability Act.

13. Expand access to health insurance.

14. 1996.

15. Regulated health insurers.

16. Leave it to the states.

17. HIPAA requires insurers selling individual health insurance policies to provide coverage to these people, provided certain conditions are met.

18. Group.

19. Insurers selling to this market must accept every small group that applies for coverage, and they must accept every eligible individual in a group, provided she applies when she first becomes eligible.

20. Both group and individual / medical expense coverage only.

21. Consolidated Omnibus Budget Reconciliation Act.

22. 20.

23. 18; employees and their dependents; employee's.

24. Family and Medical Leave Act.

25. 12; 12.

26. • The birth, adoption, or foster care placement of a child;

    • a serious health condition that prevents the employee from performing the essential functions of her job; or

    • caring for a child, spouse, or parent with a serious health condition.

27. It requires that while an employee is on family or medical leave, she must continue to be covered by her group health insurance plan.

28. It prohibits employers from discriminating against any individual on the basis of race, color, religion, sex, or national origin with respect to compensation or the terms, conditions, or privileges of employment—including the right to participate in an employer-sponsored group health insurance plan and the terms of participation in that plan.

29. Pregnancy.

30. Both medical expense insurance and disability income insurance.

31. Must.

32. 20; 40.

33. The same amounts on all employees.

34. It bans discrimination against disabled people in employee benefits, including health insurance.

35. Credit, employment, and insurance.

36. • Information is accurate and current.

    • Only relevant information is used.

    • Confidentiality is protected.

    • Information is used in a way that is, proper and fair to individuals.

37. Aged 65 or older; with certain disabilities.

38. a.   Part A.

    b. Part B.

    c. Part A.

    d. Part B.

    e. Part A.

    f.   Both Part A and Part B.

39. For some services not covered by Part A.

40. It fills in the gaps of the benefits provided by Medicare.

41. Many group policies stipulate that dependent coverage for a spouse ends when the spouse becomes eligible for Medicare benefits.

42. Benefits first; expenses not covered by the group plan.

43. The poor.

44. Each state provides a set of benefits to the poor and, provided that the benefit package meets certain requirements, the federal government pays a portion of the cost.

45. Who qualify for public assistance; may provide benefits to others determined to be medically needy, but are not required to do so.

46. Inpatient and outpatient hospital care, physicians' services, skilled nursing home care, home health care, laboratory and X-ray services, screening and diagnosis for children under age 21, and family planning.

47. • If a state pays benefits above the minimal level required by the federal government, it may require cost sharing for these additional benefits.

    • If a state provides benefits to some who do not qualify for public assistance, it may require cost sharing of these people.

48. Persons associated with the uniformed services.

49. Members of the uniformed services, retirees from the services, and the dependents of both.

50. Medicare. (Retirees are eligible for TRICARE until they reach age 65, when they become eligible for Medicare.)

51. CHAMPUS.

52. These people must sometimes receive health care services from civilian providers, and TRICARE pays benefits for these services.

53. It helps cover the deductibles and coinsurance that TRICARE beneficiaries receive.

PRACTICE EXAM QUESTIONS

This section is intended to familiarize the student with the format of AHIP examinations. If you would like to take an online pretest for *Fundamentals of Health Insurance, Part B*, visit *www.insuranceeducation.org*.

1. Bobby is 12 years old. He is covered as a dependent by both his mother's and his father's health insurance policies. His parents are married. If Bobby incurs a loss covered by both policies, which policy will be considered primary under coordination of benefits? (Assume both policies have COB provisions.)

    a. His father's policy.

    b. His mother's policy.

    c. The policy of the older parent.

    d. The policy of the parent whose birthday falls earlier in the year.

2. Centers of excellence are primarily intended for patients with

    a. difficult-to-treat or rare illnesses.

    b. drug or alcohol dependency.

    c. nursing care needs.

    d. terminal illnesses.

3. A claim examiner questions the attending physician's report for a disability claimant. What does the insurer have the right to do?

    a. The insurer can require more information from the attending physician, but it may not require an additional examination.

    b. The insurer can require an additional examination by another physician selected by the claimant.

    c. The insurer can require an additional examination by another physician agreed to by both the claimant and the insurer.

    d. The insurer can require an additional examination by another physician selected by the insurer.

4. For which of these is experience rating most likely to be used?

    a. A large group.

    b. A medium-size group.

    c. A small group.

    d. An individual.

5. Which of the following statements best describes the impact of case management on cost control?

    a. Case management is appropriate only in a few cases, but it can save a lot of money in those cases.

    b. Case management is appropriate only in a few cases, and it can save only a moderate amount of money in those cases.

    c. Case management is appropriate in many cases, and it can save a lot of money in those cases.

    d. Case management is appropriate in many cases, but it can save only a moderate amount of money in those cases.

6. Generally, group health insurance policies have

    a. annual premiums.

    b. monthly premiums.

    c. quarterly premiums.

    d. semi-annual premiums.

7. What health insurance policies does HIPAA require insurers to renew?

    a. All group health insurance policies and all individual medical expense policies, but not individual policies for other health coverages.

    b. All health insurance policies, both group and individual.

    c. All individual health insurance policies and all group medical expense policies, but not group policies for other health coverages.

    d. All medical expense policies, both group and individual, but not policies for other health coverages.

8. Hospice care focuses on

I.   addressing the patient's emotional and spiritual needs.

II. prolonging the patient's life.

III. relieving the patient's pain and discomfort.

a. I and II only.

b. I and III only.

c. II and III only.

d. I, II, and III.

9. Inspectors from a state insurance department conducting an examination of an insurer have the right to

I.   inspect the company's records.

II. interrogate the company's agents and employees.

III. interrogate the company's officers.

a. I and II only.

b. I and III only.

c. II and III only.

d. I, II, and III.

10. An insurer _____ the right to decline to renew a health insurance policy.

a. always has

b. never has

c. usually does not have

d. usually has

11. In most group health insurance plans, what is the employer charged for a group member who was covered for part of the month being billed for but who is not covered as of the premium due date?

a. A prorated amount.

b. Half the full monthly amount.

c. Nothing.

d. The full monthly amount.

12. Most states require that when an individual policy is reinstated, coverage must be provided for an illness that begins

    a. after the end of the grace period and before reinstatement.

    b. after the date of reinstatement.

    c. more than 10 days after the date of reinstatement.

    d. more than 31 days after the date of reinstatement.

13. Which statement best describes federal government efforts to combat health insurance fraud?

    a. The FBI conducts all anti-fraud activities of the federal government.

    b. Federal anti-fraud activities are conducted primarily by such agencies as the Department of Health and Human Services, and the FBI has very little involvement.

    c. The FBI conducts some federal anti-fraud activities, but other federal agencies handle some types of fraud, and the FBI has no involvement or authority in these areas.

    d. The FBI conducts some federal anti-fraud activities, and other federal agencies handle some types of fraud, but the FBI works with these other agencies and has the authority to investigate all types of fraud.

14. The state of Murcia has some laws that are extraterritorial. If an insurer headquartered in the state of Lusitania sells a policy to a resident of Murcia, the policy will be subject to

    a. all the laws of Lusitania and all the laws of Murcia.

    b. all the laws of Lusitania and none of the laws of Murcia.

    c. all the laws of Lusitania and the extraterritorial laws of Murcia.

    d. none of the laws of Lusitania, only the extraterritorial laws of Murcia.

15. A surgeon bills for several procedures as if she had performed them separately, when in fact she performed them as part of one operation. This billing scheme is known as

    a. billing for noncovered treatments.

    b. billing for services not provided.

    c. unbundling of charges.

    d. upcoding.

16. There are six components of the necessary amount of a premium. To obtain the premium amount, five of these components are added, and one is subtracted. Which one is subtracted?

    a. Investment income.

    b. Margin.

    c. Profit.

    d. Reserves.

17. In which of these rating methods do rates *not* go up with age?
    I.   Attained-age rating.
    II. Entry-age rating.
    III. Level rating.

    a. I and II only.

    b. I and III only.

    c. II and III only.

    d. I, II, and III.

18. Which statement most accurately reflects the trends of recent years?

    a. The number of people with health insurance has grown, and the number of people without health insurance has declined.

    b. The number of people with health insurance has declined, and the number of people without health insurance has grown.

    c. The number of people with health insurance and the number of people without health insurance have both grown.

    d. The number of people with health insurance and the number of people without health insurance have both declined.

19. Which statement best describes the trend in special investigative units (SIUs)?

    a. SIUs are becoming more common, but most insurers still do not have them.

    b. SIUs are becoming more common, and most insurers now have them.

    c. SIUs are becoming less common, but most insurers still have them.

    d. SIUs are becoming less common, and few insurers still have them.

20. Typically, an insured must submit a notice of claim in writing within _____ days after a loss or as soon thereafter as reasonably possible.

    a. 5

    b. 20

    c. 60

    d. 90

Answers

The chapter number of the question is in parentheses.

1. d (7)		**11.** c (4)	
2. a(10)		**12.** c (7)	
3. d (8)		**13.** d (12)	
4. a(14)		**14.** c (15)	
5. a (10)		**15.** c (11)	
6. b (4)		**16.** a (13)	
7. d (17)		**17.** c (14)	
8. b (10)		**18.** c (9)	
9. d (16)		**19.** b (12)	
10. c (3)		**20.** b (6)	